GOING WITH THE FLOW - A WALK ALONG THE NÎMES AQUEDUCT

BRIAN SOUTHGATE

GOING WITH THE FLOW
A WALK ALONG THE NÎMES AQUEDUCT

With photographs by James Colledge

© 1st Edition, 2021

ISBN: 9798531064554

Dedication:

To my beloved Pat with thanks for her tolerance as I dragged her around the garrigue looking at overgrown ditches and piles of rocks. Whether she shared any of my interest or just wanted to keep me company, I will never know. But she never complained bless her.

Tot aquarum tam multis necessariis molibus pyramidas videlicet otiosas compares aut cetera inertia sed fama celebrate opera Graecorum

I ask you! Just compare the vast monuments of this vital aqueduct network to those useless Pyramids, or the good-for-nothing tourist attractions of the Greeks!

Sextus Julius Frontinus, De Aquaeductu

What have the Romans ever done for us?

(From '*Monty Python's Life of Brian*' ©)

Reg: *They've bled us white, the bastards. They've taken everything we had, not just from us, from our fathers and from our fathers' fathers. And what have they ever given us in return?*

Xerxes: *The aqueduct?*

Reg: *Oh yeah, yeah, they gave us that. Yeah. That's true.*

Contents

List of figures and photographs

1. Introduction

I first saw the Pont du Gard in the early 1970's having 'accidentally' diverted my father via Remoulins on a holiday trip from the UK to Spain. In those days you could park your car for free, climb up into the water channel and scramble out through the missing slabs and on to the top of the bridge. This I did until my mother shrieked 'Our Brian, get down NOW!'.

A few years later, now a (relatively) sensible adult, I remember looking wistfully beyond the channel to the north into the overgrown garrigue and thinking, 'If this is an aqueduct, where is the rest of it?'.

It took me many years, much research, several holiday trips, and a very tolerant partner to find the beginning and the end of the aqueduct, the basics of its route and some of the more prominent vestiges along its winding way from Uzès to Nîmes.

In 2017 I came to live in the Gard at least partly driven by a growing obsession to find more of the aqueduct and to follow its entire course. This book is a culmination of that obsession, aided and abetted by my photographically skilled and dry-witted friend James Colledge, and by my faithful and sometimes manic labradollie Cookie.

There is no doubt that the Pont du Gard is a magnificent structure, located in a beautiful setting. It shows just what the Romans were capable of in terms of the construction of spectacular buildings and great feats of engineering. However, this bridge is only one of several along the Nîmes aqueduct and it makes up less than 1% of its total length and it is the whole of the aqueduct that this guide is really about.

James and I have spent over four years searching for the slightest trace of any of the other vestiges of the aqueduct with some very satisfying results and rewards, and a good deal of frustration. I hope that you can use this guide to get as much interest and excitement as we did in finding the smallest of vestiges hidden in the undergrowth, because that is what 'going with the flow' is all about. But please remember that to an archaeologist a stone is a stone, two stones are two stones, and three dressed stones in a row are a wall or, if you are going with the flow, a vestige of the aqueduct.

If you decide to follow this guide there are a few things that I think that you should bear in mind. Firstly, that the 50 km of the aqueduct was built and maintained without many of the tools that we now take for granted. The picks and chisels that the Romans used were made of very soft iron and required continual reworking and sharpening to allow them to make an impression on the limestone that dominates the geology between Uzès and Nîmes. Also, the surveying equipment, if that is not too strong a word to use, was crude in the extreme. When we consider that the average fall of the aqueduct was rarely greater than 1/4 of a millimetre for each metre of its length, the Roman equivalent of the spirit level, the *chlorobates,* was a 6 metre long plank of wood with a longitudinal groove filled with water. It is hard to imagine of this as a piece of precision equipment capable of measuring such miniscule slopes. And there was the *groma*, used to survey straight lines and right angles; an unwieldy contraption of strings and weights which would be set into motion by the slightest breath of wind. And finally, the *dioptra*, an optical device without any real optics which was a simple sighting tube used to check angles over long distances.

And as if the paucity of the equipment did not make the job hard enough, we must remember that in the 1st century CE much of the course of the aqueduct would have been through thickly wooded terrain covered with dense spikey undergrowth. The climate too would have been much the same as it is today; very hot and bone dry for many months of the year. Would you have wanted to work in those situations and under those conditions just to supply clean fresh water to the homes and bath houses of the more well-heeled residents of Nemausus (the Roman name for Nîmes)? As you walk casually through the garrigue with your engineered walking poles and bottles of fresh water try to imagine working there under the conditions that pertained 2,000 years ago.

What I found amazing is just how much of the aqueduct remains relatively intact so long after it was constructed. Having said that, much of what remains is underground and is protected from the elements and the depredations of the stone robbers who 'recycled' much of the above ground stonework. Dressed Roman stone was used in the Middle Ages in the construction of many buildings near to the route of the aqueduct. Then there was the wholesale destruction of large section of the aqueduct during the abortive attempts to create the Canal de Pouzin in the 19th century.

What is of serious concern are the effects of the last few decades of quarrying and house construction, and the general neglect of the aqueduct. Many vestiges that were easily found only a few years ago are now destroyed or so badly overgrown as to be almost impossible to find. Notwithstanding, the author and his comrades (human and canine) have located almost 100 vestiges of various sizes which together make the course of the aqueduct a fascinating walk. But beware! Even over the short period that James and I have been exploring the aqueduct some vestiges have disappeared or have become inaccessible; the aqueduct will not last for ever.

On a personal note, I would have loved to have been able to peer into one of the regards and see the water flowing past on its way from Uzés to Nîmes, something that it did 24 hours a day, 365 days a year, for so many decades. Sadly, like me wanting to be an astronaut or to score a goal for Manchester United against Liverpool, this is a dream that I will never realise. But walking along the course of the aqueduct through the wonderful Gardoise landscape is a very acceptable consolation, especially as it is now my home.

Brian Southgate

December 2021

About the photographer: In 1965 at the age of 12, James Colledge managed to get an entry included in the annual senior school's arts exhibition that year: a picture of le Pont du Gard, which he had developed and printed himself. From those early days he has taken photos more or less constantly, through a long journey from Scotland to his current home in Uzès, a stone's throw from the aforementioned monument.

He met the Author shortly after moving there permanently in 2015, quickly recognising their mutual though different interests in l'Aqueduc de Nîmes. He has since taken over 1,700 pictures of the vestiges, of which the few chosen by Brian, adorn this book.

His black and white series 'Repérages/Waypoints: l'Aqueduc de Nîmes' was successfully exhibited in Vers-Pont-du-Gard in July 2021. The series can be seen on his website, https://www.jamescolledgephotography.com/laqueduc-de-nimes.

2. A historical context

This book is not intended to be a historical account of the construction and operation of the Nîmes aqueduct, many authors have done a much better job of that than I ever could. However, it would be remiss of me not to include some historic context, especially where it will help in the appreciation of the vestiges that I hope you will find.

Notwithstanding Monty Pythons *'Life of Brian'©*, every schoolboy and schoolgirl knows how important water was to the Romans and how much it contributed to the everyday life of their citizens by way of their sanitary arrangements. Frontinus, the curator of Rome's many aqueducts in the 1st century, claimed that the maintenance of aqueducts was 'the best testimony to the greatness of the Roman empire'. The remains of bath houses are visible at almost every permanent settlement across the Roman empire and those bath houses were as important to the social and political lives of forts, towns, and cities as they were in keeping the populace reasonably clean, at least by the standards of 2,000 years ago. And bath houses required a plentiful supply of clean water which could not always be supplied by static wells, hence the need for aqueducts of which over 600 are known to exist in the Roman world.

When we look at a structure like the Nîmes aqueduct, its walls, bridges and tunnels, several questions come to mind:

- When was it built?
- How long did it take to build?
- Who built it?
- How much did it cost?
- How long did it operate for?

Many archaeologists, much more knowledgeable than I am, cannot agree on the answers to any of these questions. For example, it is not known with any certainty when the aqueduct was built or how long it took to build it. One school of thought says that its construction commenced around 19 BCE and is credited to Marcus Vipsanius Agrippa. Agrippa was son-in-law and lieutenant of the emperor Augustus who had been responsible for a campaign of building and improving public works in the empire. This included the construction of many aqueducts notably the Aqua Julia, Rome's fifth aqueduct. However, excavations suggest that the Nîmes aqueduct was actually constructed between 40 and 60 CE. Agrippa died in 12 BCE and the reign of Augustus was over in 14 CE so these later estimates would put construction of the aqueduct during the reign of the emperor Claudius (41–54 CE).

The cost of construction is equally uncertain together with how it was financed. In his lovely book 'The aqueduct of Nemausus' (© Published by McFarland and Company Inc. ISBN 0-89950-277-6, 1988) George Hauck estimates a total cost of 5 million sesterces, this being 5,000 worker-years with an average annual wage of 1,000 sesterces. This works out at about 100,000 sesterces per kilometre, a value typical of other major aqueducts in the Roman empire. Translating this into modern day money is difficult but a very rough estimate can be made. If we assume that four first century sesterceses had approximately the same buying power as a twenty first century euro, this gives a total cost of about 1.25 million euros in today's money.

As is the case for the date of construction the period for which the aqueduct operated is the subject of much discussion resulting in a wide range of estimates for its useful lifetime. A measurable feature is the build-up of calcium deposits (calcretions) on the walls of the aqueduct channel, but this also depends on the rate of water flow which is known to have varied significantly over the working life of the aqueduct. The lowest estimate for the life of the fully operational aqueduct (i.e. taking water the full distance from Uzès to Nîmes) is about 150 years. Some have estimated life spans of up to 800 years although this is likely to apply only to discreet sections such as to the south and east of Uzès where the aqueduct was mainly underground and may have provided local irrigation water long after the supply to Nîmes ceased.

It has been estimated that the aqueduct originally supplied Nemausus with between 35 and 40 thousand cubic metres of water a day. The water took between 24 and 30 hours to flow from the source to the castellum at a speed of between 1.0 and 1.7 metres per second. The flow rate gradually reduced over the years, mainly due to increasing losses through leakage and the build-up of calcretions within the channel. It has been estimated that the flow rate may have been less than 10 thousand cubic metres per day towards the end of the operational life of the aqueduct.

History has a habit of repeating itself and this is particularly true in the case of the water supply to the city of Nîmes. In the nineteenth century, many centuries after the Roman aqueduct had fallen into disuse (and had been largely dismantled), the water supplied by the springs in Nîmes was once again proving inadequate for the growing population of the city. Several projects were proposed and studied including that proposed by the Marquis de Preigne in 1852. His scheme was for a 102 km long canal to bring water from the Rhone at Pouzin in the Ardèche to Nîmes at a cost of 24 million Francs. The water was to be carried along a 2.8 metre diameter cast iron pipe laid in a channel 3.0 metres high and 4.0 metres wide. The course of the 'Canal de Pouzin' joined that of the Roman aqueduct in the region of the Pont Roupt, passed over the Pont du Gard, through the Bois de Remoulins by way of a series of cuttings and tunnels, and then approximately followed the course of its predecessor to Nîmes. The project was launched in May 1863 with huge fanfare and a massive banquet on the Pont du Gard. The construction work itself commenced with the drilling of a tunnel at the southern end of the bridge, on the same level as the Roman water channel. This was followed by the excavation of a wide trench just before the Pont de Valmale, other excavations in Saint Bonnet du Gard, Lédenon, Bezouce and Nîmes, and the construction of immense brick built galleries between Marguerittes and Courbessac. For some of its course the canal ran close to the Roman aqueduct without significant disturbance, but in the region of Saint Bonnet du Gard and after Bezouce it was constructed on almost precisely the same course, destroying much of the Roman aqueduct in the process. By March 1868 the project was abandoned after the excavation of about 10 km of trench and the construction of about 1 km of underground galleries, barely 10% of the projected total.

Today the canal is mainly backfilled although some of the trenches and the brick built chambers and massive regards remain, particularly between Marguerittes and Courbessac. Some of the owners of the land where the brick built sections are located have restored the chambers for various uses including, at one time, the growing of mushrooms. There is a rumour that during the German occupation of Southern France in World War 2 the French Resistance used the subterranean parts of the canal for hiding themselves and their weapons. Then again, another rumour suggests that the Wehrmacht used the chambers as ammunition dumps.

3. The course of the aqueduct

The location of the Roman city of Nemausus was not optimal when it came to providing a bulk water supply. The city was surrounded by plains to the south and the east and these were of insufficient elevation to provide a usable 'head' of water pressure. The hills to the west would have made the route of an aqueduct too difficult from an engineering point of view and therefore too expensive. The only real option was to bring the water from the north, specifically from the area to the east of the small town of Ucetia, now Uzès, where plentiful clean water was available from several perennial springs.

The distance as the crow flies from Uzès to Nîmes is about 20 km, but water does not have the same ability as a crow and can only flow downhill. Added to this are the consequences of the geography and geology of the Gardois garrigue, notably the often precipitous gorge of the Gardon, on the feasibility of building an aqueduct along a direct line between Uzés and Nîmes. This resulted in a roughly V-shaped and serpentine course for the aqueduct approximately 50 km long. A more direct route could have been attempted but this would have required a tunnel about 10 km long which the Romans must have deemed impractical, even impossible, to construct.

The source was located in what are now the grounds of the Chateau de Plantéry to the east of Uzès. The aqueduct initially proceeded almost due south in the direction of Nîmes, along the valley of the River Alzon. After a few kilometres it turned to the southeast passing through the modern day communes of St Maximin and Argilliers, before passing to the north and east of Vers-Pont-du-Gard.

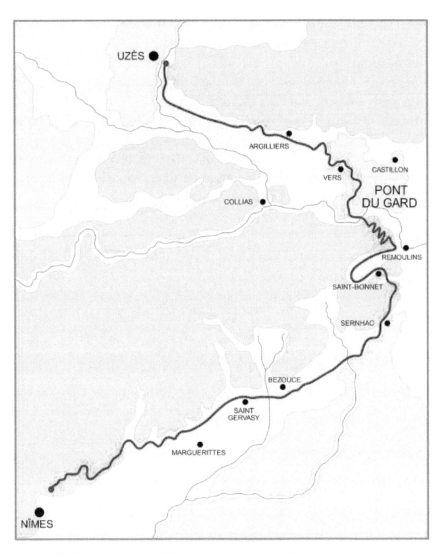

Figure 1.   The course of the Nîmes aqueduct

The aqueduct then headed due south again for a few kilometres until it reached the gorge of the Gardon where it returned to a south-eastern heading to cross the river. After the Pont du Gard the aqueduct wriggled its way through the valleys in the Bois de Remoulins before making a sharp right hand turn followed by a lazy S to take it through the area now occupied by Saint-Bonnet-du-Gard and on to Sernhac. After Sernhac the aqueduct headed south-west towards Nîmes, passing through the communes of Bezouce, St Gervasy, and to the north of Marguerittes, before it entered the walled city of Nemausus from the north-east.

4. The form of the aqueduct

It is useful at this stage to describe the basic form of the aqueduct and how it was constructed in the various types of landscape between Uzès and Nîmes. This will allow the vestiges to be more easily identified and understood.

Figure 2 shows the basic construction of the aqueduct channel which comprises a broad foundation raft, or *hérisson,* on which two stone walls were placed.

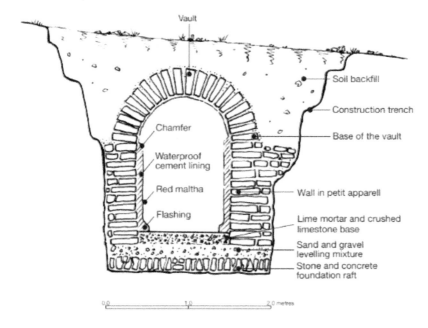

Figure 2.   Components of the aqueduct channel

The foundation raft comprised a stone and concrete base, 0.25 metres thick, on top of which was a 0.20 metre thick layer of a levelling mixture of sand, gravel, and lime. The walls were generally

19

built from unshaped stones set in cement and had a thickness of between 0.3 and 0.5 metres. The walls were usually surmounted by a vaulted roof made from flat wedge shaped stones although in a few places, notably at the Pont du Gard, flat stone slabs were used.

The internal dimensions of the water channel were a width of 1.2 metres and a height, to the underside of the centre of the vaulted roof, of 1.8 metres. This height allowed the average Roman to walk along the channel without bumping his head too often on the underside of the vault.

Photograph 1. Internal view of the aqueduct (Waypoint 22)

The lower part of the internal surfaces of the channel walls were lined with waterproof cement (*opus signinum*), a mixture of lime cement and crushed tile, with a thickness of a few centimetres. The top edges of the wall linings were finished with a chamfered bevel. The lining on the base was cast separately from the sides and comprised a 0.10 metre thick layer of lime cement containing crushed limestone. The joints between the base and wall cement were sealed with cement flashing in a roughly quadrant shape.

The wetted surfaces of the channel were painted with olive oil and covered with red *maltha*, a mixture of slaked lime, pork grease and the viscous juice of unripe figs. The maltha was possibly used to enhance the waterproofing of the channel and/or to improve the smoothness of the wetted surfaces to improve the water flow rates. However, some archaeologists doubt its efficacy for either of these functions and suspect that it might have been sold to the construction bosses by an enterprising salesman.

Each of the components of the aqueduct channel described above, even traces of the red maltha, are visible somewhere along the length of the aqueduct.

The external finish of the aqueduct depended on its location. Significant sections are of the 'cut and cover' design (Figure 2) where a trench was dug into the ground, the channel constructed therein, and the trench backfilled with earth and sub-soil after the vault was completed. Where the soil was too shallow, or non-existent, the trench was cut into the limestone bedrock. In extreme cases, and only at Sernhac and the Saint-Luc area of Nîmes, tunnels were driven through the limestone and the aqueduct built inside them.

In some places, notably to the east and south of Uzès and in the Bois de Remoulins, the aqueduct was formed by cutting back the face of the hillside to produce a vertical surface, using the rock face as one wall of the channel, and adding an L-shaped base and stone-faced wall on the downhill side.

Where the geography resulted in the aqueduct being above ground the channel was built on top of a rock shelf, a wall, an arcade of arches, or a bridge, the most spectacular example of the latter being the Pont du Gard.

For sections of the aqueduct that were above ground the external surfaces of the walls were faced with dressed stones covering a core on undressed stones. It should be noted that the facing stones were not baked clay bricks but discrete pieces of limestone individually hand-cut to the required size and shape.

Ultimately the choice of the manner of construction of the different parts of the aqueduct was made by a *mensor,* (or surveyor) who was responsible for defining the course of the aqueduct, based on cost (i.e. construction man-hours and materials) and/or making the best use of limited 'fall' of the aqueduct as a whole.

Along the length of the aqueduct were numerous 'regards' or manholes which permitted access to the channel for inspection and cleaning. Several of these can still be found, notably to the south of Sernhac. There are also two known regulator basins, one shortly after the beginning of the aqueduct near Uzès and the other on the upstream side of the Pont du Gard (the former is beautifully displayed, but the latter was backfilled after being excavated). These were used to control the amount of water entering the aqueduct to avoid overfilling (i.e. above the level of the waterproof cement) or, in the case of the Pont du Gard, overflowing the channel.

The gradient of the aqueduct channel was a key feature, indeed a major restraint, on the design and construction of the aqueduct. The total fall of just over 12 metres between the source and castellum equates to an average gradient of 0.025% which is much lower than that typically found in Roman aqueducts. And this value is an average as in places, notably after the Pont du Gard, it was sometimes as low as 0.002%. One reason for the variation in the gradient along the aqueduct's route is that a uniform gradient would have meant that the Pont du Gard would have had to be approximately 6 metres higher had the upstream section not had a larger gradient. Also, other bridges upstream of the Pont du Gard (such as at Bornègre and Roc Plan) would have had to be higher and several of the underground sections between Uzès and Vers would have had to have been supported by walls or arches, again leading to extra complexity and cost.

The water from the springs at Uzès is clear but high in dissolved calcium salts leached out of the native limestone by slightly acidic rainwater. On exposure to the atmosphere, dissolved calcium salts would have precipitated out of the water and attached themselves to the inner walls of the aqueduct channel. This deposition was progressive along the length of the aqueduct and, over time, caused the flow of water to become progressively reduced. This presented the Romans, who knew little about water chemistry, with an unexpected but significant problem in maintaining the flow of water along the aqueduct.

The build-up of 'calcretions' (sometimes referred to as 'sinter') first becomes obvious at Bornègre and by the time the aqueduct reaches the Bois de Remoulins it has blocked over half of the cross sectional area of the channel. Calcretions are also apparent where the aqueduct channel leaked, and they were either deposited on the

23

external walls (known as 'curtain calcretions') or accumulated as huge blocks alongside the aqueduct or underneath the arches.

Another threat to the quality of the water delivered by the aqueduct was posed by the roots of vegetation penetrating the vault of the channel. The presence of such roots introduced algae and bacteria and their decomposition, by a process called biolithogenesis, could contaminate the previously pure spring water. Clearing roots and other vegetable matter required constant maintenance by the workers responsible for the aqueduct's upkeep, who accessed the channel by way of regards and scrubbed the walls and the underside of the vault clear of vegetation.

5. How to use this guide

The main purpose of this guide is to share the interest and pleasure that the Author and his companions have gained from their extended exploration of the Nîmes aqueduct, as well as to allow the user to enjoy the countryside along the way.

Had the Romans intended to create a challenging walk with both interest and beauty they would have struggled to do a better job than that provided by the route of the Nîmes aqueduct. At times you will see little or no evidence of the aqueduct but then you will turn a corner and see one of the many pieces of the aqueduct appearing out of the undergrowth.

Part of the reason for the lack of visible aqueduct stonework is that, as mentioned earlier, a considerable proportion of the channel was constructed underground. However, all is not lost as there are many examples where the course of the aqueduct has created the basis for more recent field boundaries, usually in the form of a bank and parallel sunken area. My own theory for this is that when the trench was dug to permit the construction of the aqueduct the spoil was piled up alongside and some of this now remains. The sunken area corresponds to places where the refilled trench has settled or the aqueduct has collapsed.

Sadly, it is not possible to follow the whole course of the aqueduct as, for example, one can follow the route of Hadrian's Wall in northern England. Whilst much of the route is well known some of it passes through private property, both agricultural and residential. I have experienced no problems with either but in both cases personal property and privacy should be respected. This can be frustrating, no more so than in the Roc Plan area of Vers-Pont-du-Gard where an exquisite trio of arches form the backdrop to a private garden (I say with much envy!).

This guide has been written in such a manner that the user can follow the course of the aqueduct as closely as is practicable, avoiding main roads wherever possible, and see all the visible vestiges that are still extant and accessible. If you follow the route as described in this book you will rarely be more than 100 metres from the course of the aqueduct, and usually a good deal closer.

Regarding the course of the aqueduct and the location of the many vestiges, I have made extensive use of the magnificent tome: *L'aqueduc de Nîmes et le Pont du Gard* (© published by the Centre National de la Recherche Scientifique, Centre d'études Préhistoire Antiquité Moyen Âge ISBN 2-271-05731-0, 2001). This book includes a set of 16 maps covering the entire length of the aqueduct, together with nearly 200 locations (referred to herein as 'Waypoints') at which vestiges were known to exist when the book was first published in the late 1990s, or for which archaeological records exist. The numbering and naming system for these Waypoints is followed in this guide and a set of simplified maps have been produced.

Our explorations have located a total of approximately 5 km of walls, arcades, mounds, and trenches which are remains of the aqueduct. A simple sum shows that this means that about 90% of the aqueduct is no longer visible. A good proportion of this 'missing' portion is underground, notably to the south-east of Uzès and between Sernhac and Nîmes, where the occasional channel collapse, regard or modern day excavation is all that can be seen. Also, the efforts of the Marquis de Preigne in building the Canal de Pouzin resulted in the destruction of at least 10 km of the aqueduct. So, whilst this means that many kilometres will be walked without seeing any trace of the aqueduct, the principle of 'going with the flow' is that you will follow its course as closely as possible, even if it is several metres below your feet or that it was destroyed many years ago.

How you use this guide will depend on your degree of interest, for example:

- As an interested tourist, you could limit yourself to the start and end of the aqueduct but of course taking in the Pont du Gard.
- As a casual walker, you could follow the section from the source to the south of Uzès and then approach the Pont du Gard from the village of Vers, both sections having easy walking and several interesting vestiges.
- As a keen walker, the entire section between Uzès and the Pont du Gard, and the beginning of the Bois de Remoulins make a good walk.
- As an adventurous walker, the vestiges to the west and north of Vers and the whole of the Bois de Remoulins will tax you a little more.
- Or, as a fellow obsessive, a fully paid up 'aqueducteur' (or 'aqueducteuse'), you could do the lot and find every extant vestige between the source and the castellum.

The walking time for the full length of the aqueduct, including the time taken to locate all the vestiges identified in Chapter 6, is about 24 hours, which is similar to the time taken by the water to flow the same distance in antiquity. I suggest that a walk of the entire length of the aqueduct should sensibly be spread over 3 or 4 days.

At what time of year you should make the walk is a major consideration. Personally, I would recommend March or April when the weather is moderate and before the undergrowth gets too dense and some of the vestiges are concealed or impossible to reach. Also, this is a good time for seeing the wonderful flora of the garrigue, including wild cistus and irises, and a huge variety of orchids. During the summer temperatures can exceed 40°C and some of the more interesting fauna may venture out, including lizards and snakes, although very few of the latter are venomous. The temperatures are obviously gentler during the autumn and winter although the undergrowth will be at its densest and there is always the possibility of heavy rain.

Finally, some advice regarding a dress code for 'aqueducting'. Whilst many of the vestiges are approached by way of tarmacked roads or obvious paths some of the more difficult to find, notably in the Bois de Remoulins, will require you to make your way through overgrown areas which could be described as being 'impenetrable'. The undergrowth includes various wild plants which have sharp and clinging barbs. You should wear reasonably tough shoes, clothes that can bear a few rips and scratches, and carry walking poles.

6. Following the course of the aqueduct

During our explorations over the past four years we have located about 100 individual vestiges, varying from sunken areas or a few dressed stones, to massive structures such as the Pont du Gard. Figure 3 shows the locations of all of these vestiges and also indicates the overall scale of the route of the aqueduct.

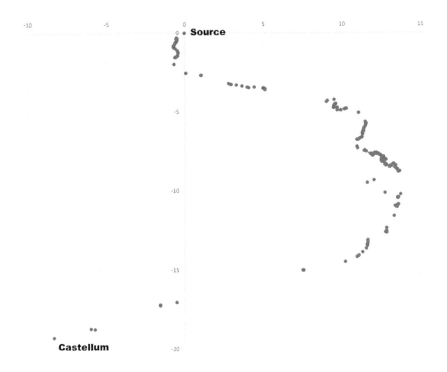

Figure 3.   The complete set of visible vestiges (Scale in km)

As it is not feasible to walk the full length of the aqueduct from the source to the castellum in a single day. Accordingly, this chapter breaks the aqueduct into eight sections, to assist in the planning of a sensible walking schedule.

Each section below commences with a reference to the relevant walking map(s) and an estimate of the distance to be walked and the time that such a walk would take. The timings are generous to allow for locating each of the extant vestiges. This is followed by a list of the vestiges that are visible in that section together with a very brief description of each.

The form of each vestige is described in the summary as:

- VS = Visible stonework
- VO = Visible 'other' (i.e. not stone, usually a ditch!).
- NA = Visible but not accessible

The commentaries that follow give more detail regarding the walking route and the location of each vestige, together with a fuller description. The numbering of the 'Waypoints' mentioned previously is used and those where visible vestiges exist being **highlighted**.

Each section includes one or more maps to give additional help in finding your way. The maps are not meant to be geographically perfect and are included to show the relative routes of the aqueduct (shown as a grey dashed line), the visible Waypoints (marked in black with their respective numbers) and the recommended walking route (shown as a black dashed line). Some significant roads and railway lines are also included. For more accurate maps to further assist you in finding your way I suggest that you obtain the *IGN Carte de Randonnée* (TOP 25) Nos. 2941 O (Uzès), 2941 E (Remoulins, Pont du Gard) and 2942 OT (Nîmes, Beaucaire).

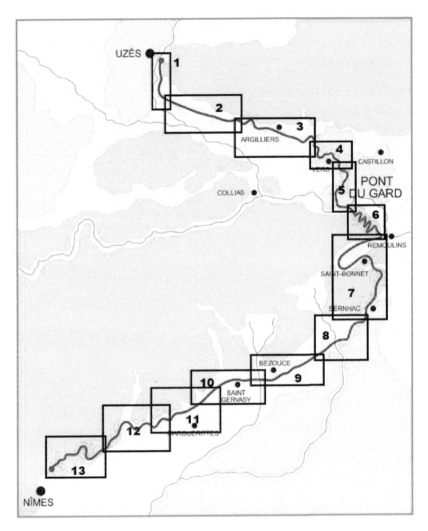

Figure 4. The full set of walking maps

References to the 'course of the aqueduct' are made irrespective of whether or not anything is visible, the aqueduct may be underground or may have been destroyed. The course of the aqueduct is that

31

determined over many years by archaeologists locating obvious vestiges and/or by deriving a route between vestiges by way of following the contours of the landscape.

Finally, since in this book we will be 'going with the flow', any references to the left and right aspects of the aqueduct are with you looking along the aqueduct in the direction of the historic flow of water (i.e. towards Nîmes). References to the left and right hand walls are to the walls of the water channel itself whereas other references to walls are generally to the supporting wall upon which the channel is located.

6.1 The Alzon valley

Map 1 - Waypoints 1 to 11

Distance: ~3 km   Walking Time: ~1½ hours

Waypoint	Form	Description
2 - Fontaine d'Eure	VS	Section of open channel
2A - Bassin de Val d'Eure	VS	Restored regulator basin and overflow channel
3 - Moulin du Tournal	VO	Aqueduct debris
4 - La Montagne	VS	Two extended sections of open channel
5	VS	100 metres of open channel
7 - Mas de Préville	VS/NA	Tunnel exit and length of channel in private garden. Cut back bedrock face outside gate of property
8 - Château Bérard	VS	Several pieces of channel wall under modern wall. 2 metre wide slot cut in bedrock
9 - Carrignargues	VS	Cut back rock face and short row of dressed stone
11 - Carrignargues	VS	Channel in limestone trench, in private garden

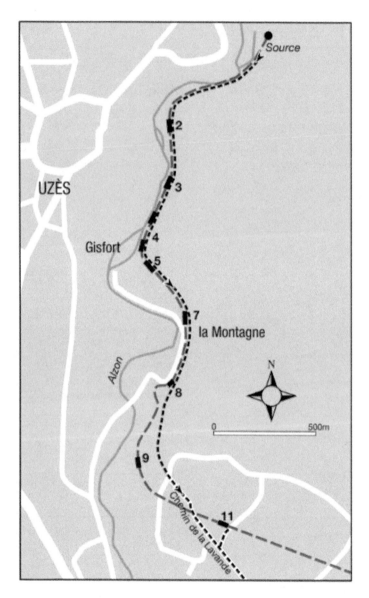

Map 1.   The Alzon valley

For the first few kilometres the aqueduct travels in a southerly direction from the source and almost directly towards Nîmes. This however is not by design but rather a constraint of the Alzon valley, sandwiched as it is between two elevated areas; that to the west occupied by the town of Uzès and la Montagne to the east. Much of this section of the aqueduct is at or close to ground level and whilst extensive robbing of dressed stone has inevitably taken place over the centuries several extensive vestiges are still visible. There is virtually no sign of calcretion in this section and, as a result, the form of the cement lining of the aqueduct channel is visible and often in very good condition.

Our route starts in the Vallée de l'Eure at the northern end of the valley carved by the Alzon river. This can be accessed by leaving Uzès on the D982 in the direction of Bagnols-sur-Cèze and turning right at the signpost after about 1km. Before you reach the car park you will see on your left the Chateau de Plantéry and then the 19th century pumphouse which bears a board claiming it to be the source of water for the Roman aqueduct.

The Fontaine de l'Eure has provided the citizens of Uzès with fresh water for many years since the construction of the Roman aqueduct having proved to be a dependable, perennial, and plentiful source. It still continues to provide water to Uzès but a steady flow still rushes from the left hand side of the pumphouse and eventually into the Alzon. The springs themselves are located in the area behind the pumphouse (Photograph 2) which is controlled by the Commune of Uzès, and access can sometimes be obtained by asking at the Mairie.

This area is a pleasure to visit particularly in the autumn when wild cyclamen surrounds the spring pool. The water is crystal clear, and you can see bubbles of air rising from the bottom as the spring water seeps into the pool.

The location of Waypoint 1, the beginning of the aqueduct, is about 100 metres to the north of the pool in the grounds the Chateau de Plantéry. Nothing from the Roman period is now visible although in the 1920s a 4 metre diameter circular structure was found. The archaeologists concluded that the water that supplied the aqueduct was probably drawn from several springs which were directed into this collection basin and thereby into the aqueduct channel.

Photograph 2. The spring pool near Chateau de Plantéry

Excavations and geophysical examinations over the last century have shown that the aqueduct proceeded alongside the left bank of the Alzon and across the modern day sports field. The walking route commences by following the path that hugs the steep bank on your left and, after you pass a stone marking the 'beginning' of the aqueduct, you will soon reach the first visible remains. However, as you approach this vestige you should note the row of trees on the right side of the path. These appear to be growing in a broad ditch which corresponds roughly to the course of the aqueduct.

There is no mistaking the first vestige of the aqueduct; a 50 metre length of channel (**Waypoint 2 - Fontaine d'Eure**) from which the vault has been removed. This leads to the regulator, a multiple sluiced arrangement for controlling the flow of water along the aqueduct (**Waypoint 2A - Bassin du Val d'Eure**).

Photograph 3. Waypoint 2A - The regulator

The regulator (Photograph 3) which was discovered, excavated, and wonderfully preserved in 1991, includes a number of vertical slots, presumably for the sluice gates, and round holes on the horizontal surfaces, possibly used to mount the operating mechanisms for the gates. To the right of the regulator is a stone-lined overflow channel about 50 metres long which allowed excess water to be returned to the Alzon.

The short length of vaulted channel visible at the entry to the regulator shows the size and the original state of the aqueduct channel. Do not resist the temptation to jump down into the regulator and walk through this piece of the complete channel, it is the one of the few opportunities that you will get to do this. Try to take away an impression of the size of the channel as this will add context when you see fragments of it later on.

If you look carefully at the cement lining of the channel you will see how well preserved it is including the flashing at the base, the bevelled top edges, and even traces of red maltha. The appearance of this latter material is rare as it would have been less robust than the cement itself and, further down the channel, it would have been covered by calcretion.

Leaving the regulator follow the tree line on your left and note the depression running alongside you. This follows the course of the aqueduct which is further evidenced by signs of past archaeological excavations. Keeping to the left you will reach the medieval Moulin du Tournal which sits on top of the aqueduct, and which may have used part of the Roman channel to provide water to the mill wheel. Sadly, the construction of the mill probably destroyed the aqueduct channel and the Roman stonework 'robbed' to provide building material. Notwithstanding, there are traces of aqueduct rubble to the south of the mill (**Waypoint 3 - Moulin du Tornal**).

Cross the wooden bridge over the old mill race and continue along the path. The aqueduct continues to hug the steep hillside and you can see where the limestone bedrock was cut back in places to form the left hand wall of the channel. This is the first example of the use of an L-shaped channel. In some places a horizontal platform has been formed from the bedrock, on which the aqueduct channel would have been built. In other places a full channel has been cut in the bedrock to accommodate the aqueduct

Photograph 4. Waypoint 4 - La Montagne

Three good sections of the aqueduct channel totalling about 200 metres exist in the Quartier Gisfort (**Waypoint 4 - La Montagne**) where you have an opportunity to walk along the channel with impunity (Photograph 4). The cement lining is still solid and in places the original toolmarks along the flashing at the bottom of the channel can be seen.

As you approach a gate posted with dire warnings about wild animals (occasionally there are bulls and horses) the aqueduct makes a 45° turn to the left and disappears into thick undergrowth. After passing through the gate you should turn left into the field and follow its edge until you reach the far side. Here you will re-discover the aqueduct as a deep trench with both walls still lined with cement right up to the bevelled tops (**Waypoint 5**). The vault has gone and the left hand wall is now used as the foundation for a field wall over a length of about 100 metres. The use of the aqueduct as the base for field boundaries is a feature that recurs wherever it is close to the surface and is often an aid in following its course where no Roman stonework is visible.

Eventually the channel, which curves gently towards the left, is filled with soil and rubble and disappears into the wooded area. A few metres further along the top of the left hand wall is visible together with a suggestion of the vault. The course of the aqueduct now passes through the wooded area and little of Waypoint 6 is visible with the exception of a piece of cut back bedrock and possible evidence for the collapsed channel filled with leaf mould.

The aqueduct channel, complete with vault, reappears in the vegetable garden of *La Magnanerie de Préville* (**Waypoint 7 - Mas de Préville**) but this section is on private land and is not accessible. It can however be seen from the field. Turn right at the end of the field, return to the track and turn left

As the course of the aqueduct enters the Quartier Préville its course is sandwiched between the Alzon on the right and a steep rock face on the left. Immediately after the gate of *La Magnanerie de Préville* and also further down the lane there are a number of examples of the rock having been cut back to form the left hand wall of the aqueduct.

As you follow the lane downhill you are effectively following the course of the aqueduct and there are several obvious sections of one wall of the aqueduct which appears at the bottom of the more recent boundary wall on the left hand side of the lane. The aqueduct stones are semi-regular and cemented in position whereas the stones that make up the boundary wall are placed on top of the aqueduct in a more random manner and without cement. Close examination of the cement in the lower section shows it to be pink in colour and containing seashells, typical of the cement used for the aqueduct. A number of exposed pieces of the cement lining are visible which suggests that we are looking at the right hand wall of the aqueduct and that the channel itself is hidden in the bank on your left. At one point some recycling of aqueduct rubble is obvious in the boundary wall, witnessed by more pink cement as well as traces of red maltha.

As you approach Château Bèrard the path begins to curve to the right whilst the course of the aqueduct turns to the left. On the right side of the path toolmarks on the rock face show where material was removed. On the left side is an obvious rectangular cut in the bedrock, about 2 metres wide, which would have accommodated the aqueduct. This opening is now filled with more recent stonework. **(Waypoint 8 - Château Bèrard)**.

The course of the aqueduct now becomes rather undefined as it continues to travel southwards but underground. Take the track on your left immediately after Waypoint 8 and climb uphill. Look at the wall on your right and you will see several pieces of aqueduct debris comprising rocks from the core of the walls, some with the cement lining still attached. The track itself is interesting in that it is deeply rutted presumably by many centuries of cartwheels. There is also evidence of ancient quarrying on the left hand side of the track.

After about 200 metres a second track joins from the left and the course of the aqueduct now crosses from left to right under the junction of the two tracks. Climb over the low wall on your right and follow the path, the course of the aqueduct is on your right hugging the steep stone face. After about 100 metres you will reach an old wooden table, on which there may be a beehive, opposite which is an opening which, after a short climb, leads to the next vestige (**Waypoint 9 - Carrignargues**). This vestige comprises a cut away rock face and a row of dressed stones. A second more substantial vestige (Waypoint 10) has been recorded in the past, about 50 metres further along, but there is no sign of it now as it is lost in the undergrowth. Shortly after Waypoint 10 the course of the aqueduct makes a 90° turn to the east, a direction it generally maintains until it reaches Vers-Pont-du-Gard.

Retrace your steps along the path and re-join the track continuing uphill. At the top of the climb turn right in front of a stone house and proceed through to a tarmac road, Chemin de la Lavande, which then becomes Chemin du Mas des Violettes.

The course of the aqueduct is about 100 metres away on your left and **Waypoint 11 - Carrignargues** is located in the garden of a house on Chemin des Arbousiers (the third house on the right, about 100 metres from Chemin du Mas des Violettes). It comprises an excavated pit in which can be seen a trench carved in the limestone bedrock together with part of the left hand wall of the aqueduct complete with the cement lining. The owner of the property, M

Messier, is a charming gentleman and is very proud of his vestige. I am sure that he would let you view it, and he will tell you all about it!

After Waypoint 11 the course of the aqueduct is not well known although if it were to follow the contours of the land it would be expected to be located between 100 and 150 metres to the left of Chemin du Mas des Violettes.

6.2 Underground to Vers-Pont-du-Gard
Maps 2 and 3 - Waypoints 12A to 36

Distance: ~10 km   Walking Time: ~3 hours

Waypoint	Form	Description
12A - Domaine de l'Aqueduc	VS	20 metres of excavated channel with traces of vault
18 - Le Castagnier	VO	Curved field boundary up to 3 metres high, total length 180 metres
19 - Les Arabades	VS	Short piece of collapsed channel
19A	VS	Restored regard
20 - Les Béringuières	VO	Sunken section, ~100 metres long
21 - La Tuilerie	VO	Ditch at edge of field
22 - La Tuilerie	VS	Tunnel exit
23 - Pont de Bornègre	VS	Three arched bridge
24 - Castille	VS	Channel crosses path and sunken trench continues into wooded area
27 - La Lèche	VO	Field boundary
28 - La Lèche	VO	Bank and rubble
33 - La Bourache	VS	Several pieces of wall, 120 metres total

Waypoint	Form	Description
34	VO	Bank along field boundary
35 - La Coste	VS	Rubble and several pieces of channel
36	VS	Several pieces of channel wall and collapsed sections

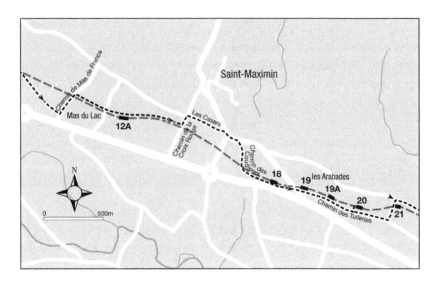

Map 2.   Saint Maximin

To the south of Uzès the direction of the aqueduct changes from southwards to eastwards and the channel disappears underground as the land rises.   The vestiges in this section are limited to the occasional collapsed channel or are the results of archaeological excavations.   Nonetheless, the route makes good walking through vines and olive trees and many of the existing field boundaries

45

appear to follow the course of the aqueduct. There is also the bonus of the Domaine de l'Aqueduc where a very pleasant range of wines can be sampled.

At the end of Chemin du Mas des Violettes turn left onto Chemin du Mas de Rey. Go past Mas du Lac on your right and after a further 150 metres, with No. 267 on your left, turn right on to the pathway between two olive orchards. You are once again walking along the course of the aqueduct although nothing obvious is visible. However, after about 100 metres there is a field boundary marked by a prominent bank and ditch. This appears to mark the course of the aqueduct and, whilst no stonework is visible, the field wall contains some dressed blocks of limestone suggesting that the stone from the aqueduct has been robbed and that it is the ditch in front of the wall that is witness to the buried aqueduct. The bank curves slightly to the right and back to the left until you reach Chemin de Mas de France. Opposite you is a large modern house under which the course of the aqueduct passes. The track on the left of the house is now more obvious and named (but not signed) Le Colombier as it continues to the east.

The next vestige can be found at the Domaine de l'Aqueduc, which can be visited by turning right down Chemin de Mas de France for about 50 metres and turn left into the winery. With the winery building on your right, continue to the picnic area and there you will find a recently excavated 15 metre section of aqueduct channel (**Waypoint 12A**).

This vestige (Photograph 5) displays both walls, to their full height and with the cement lining almost completely intact, it is only missing the vault roof, which may have been removed during excavation, or had previously collapsed into the channel. There are some signs of calcretion on the walls but, since the calcium salts in the water flowing through this section would still have been mainly in solution, these are only minor.

Photograph 5. Waypoint 12A - Domaine de l'Aqueduc

The course of the aqueduct continues eastwards and you should follow the path on the right of the exposed channel and through the next field before climbing up to your left to re-join Le Colombier.

If you have taken the more abstemious route directly along Le Colombier, after about 100 metres you will see the excavated channel on your right behind the winery.

Continue along Le Colombier for a further 100 metres and you will see a row of olive trees on your right. This marks the location Waypoint 13 although little or nothing is visible now, this being limited to ploughed up cement found in an earlier survey. If you rummage around under the large tree on your right there is a pile of suspicious rubble some of which may have come from the destruction of the aqueduct.

The track now swings to the left and the course of the aqueduct to the right. Go past a large metal gate on your left and then turn right to walk along the edge of a field of vines. Waypoint 14 is immediately on your right although nothing is now visible. The course of the aqueduct follows the edge of the field turning left after about 50 metres where there is a significant bank where the field boundary appears to follow the course of the aqueduct.

After a further 100 metres the track turns to the right and then to the left, you have crossed the course of the aqueduct and the bank which conceals it is now on your left. The bank curves gently to the south and back to the east before reaching Chemin de la Croix Rouge. Waypoint 15 is located here, previously evidenced by rubble from the aqueduct which is no longer visible.

The course of the aqueduct crosses the road and Waypoints 16 and 17 are lost in the fields in front of you and through which there is no obvious path. Instead, you should turn left and walk up Chemin de la Croix Rouge and into the village of Saint-Maximin. After about 200 metres turn right on to Chemin Neuf (D305) and proceed for about 200 metres until you reach a junction. Turn right on to Chemin des Casers (D365) and right again after about 60 metres on to Chemin de Coudières.

After about 100 metres the track swings to the left and now follows the course of the aqueduct for about 120 metres until the latter turns to the left. Follow the track for another 60 metres and turn left immediately before the D981. After a further 60 metres turn left along a field boundary and right again after 20 metres.

Ahead of you is a curved field boundary which follows the course of the aqueduct and where debris has been found in the past (Waypoint 18 - Le Castagnier). At the end of the bank, take the opening towards the main road and follow path on your left. Once again, the course of the aqueduct is indicated by the bank on your left.

After 200 metres, cross the junction on to Chemin des Tuileries and a short section of collapsed aqueduct channel can be seen in the bank on your left (**Waypoint 19 - Les Arabades**). The bank on the left hand side of the road conceals the aqueduct for about 50 metres. Continue along this road for another 250 metres and turn left on to the track called Les Arabades. After 10 metres you will see a beautifully restored regard (Photograph 6), which shows that the aqueduct is about 5 meters below ground level at this point (**Waypoint 19A**).

Photograph 6.   Waypoint 19A

Return to Chemin des Tuileries and proceed a further 200 metres, turning left up a track opposite the Route de Remoulins. After 60 metres, under a row of trees on your right, is a very distinct straight and parallel sided ditch, 1.2 metres wide, this is the collapsed aqueduct. (**Waypoint 20 - Les Béringuières**).

Return again to Chemin des Tuileries and turn left. The course of the aqueduct runs parallel to the road and about 50 metres to your left. Turn left after about 300 metres and after a further 100 metres, just before a prominent bank, in the ditch on your right you will see a collection of rubble formed when the aqueduct was damaged when the ditch was cut (**Waypoint 21 - La Tuilerie**). Climb over the ditch and follow the bank into the lightly wooded area and you will see the outline of another piece of parallel sided ditch similar to that seen at Waypoint 21.

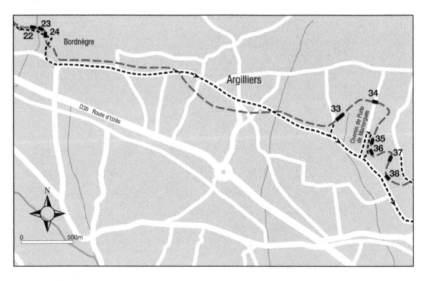

Map 3.   Argilliers

50

Return to the road and continue uphill for another 100 metres before turning right into Chemin de Bornègre. After descending a stony path, look to your left and you will see a trench leading to the exit of the aqueduct channel from the hillside (**Waypoint 22** - Photograph 7).

Photograph 7. Waypoint 22

This is one of the few opportunities to look along a section of underground channel, which stretches as far as a torch will illuminate it. This location shows the 'cut and cover' approach that was used for much of the aqueduct in this area; the excavation of a trench, building the channel and backfilling. It is also the first example of significant calcretions on the channel walls, the water having been exposed to the air long enough for the calcium salts to start coming out of solution and deposit on the walls.

The next vestige (**Waypoint 23 - Pont de Bornègre**) is the first bridge of the aqueduct, a three arch structure built to allow the seasonal Ruisseau de Bornègre to pass underneath the aqueduct (Photograph 8). The mensor clearly recognised the power of this stream which flushes like the cistern of a WC when the chamber high up in the garrigue fills with rainwater.

Photograph 8. Waypoint 23 - Pont de Bornègre

Three large arches, the outer two now being blocked, with cutwaters on the upstream sides of the pillars, seem rather excessive for a stream that, at worst, appears a trickle and which for most of the year is dry. But if you look into the stream bed you can see from the size of the rocks that have been carried downstream by the flow that it can be ferocious after a heavy storm. Indeed, the central arch still serves an important purpose in allowing the waters to run down the valley into the Alzon and eventually into the Gardon. If, as is likely, the stream is dry when you visit, search YouTube© for 'Bornègre' to see some spectacular videos of the stream in full flow.

Like many Roman legacies the bridge was used for wheeled traffic for many years after the aqueduct fell into disuse. All traces of the aqueduct channel have been removed and the stones on the tops on the arches are deeply rutted presumably by metal rimmed cartwheels. This area is a personal favourite of mine, a great place for a picnic and to let Cookie rampage through the undergrowth chasing imaginary sangliers.

Whilst you are here do not be satisfied by looking at the tunnel exit and the bridge, there is more to be seen. After passing over the bridge the course of the aqueduct goes into the undergrowth on your left but as you follow the path towards the east look down at your feet and after about 100 metres you will see a distinctive pair of 'tramlines' with a spacing of ~1.2m (**Waypoint 24 - Castille**). This indicates that the aqueduct has made a 90° bend to the right somewhere in the wooded area on your left. If you examine this vestige carefully you will see the rubble outer walls, the cement lining and the laminated calcretions (Photograph 9). The channel continues to the right of the path, evidenced by a southward heading sunken trench which extends for about 10 metres into the undergrowth.

The course of the aqueduct now swings back to the east although its exact track has been lost as it passes through an orchard of olive and oak trees (the latter being used to cultivate truffles a speciality of the area). Follow the path up the hill from Bornègre turning right at the junction. At some point you will cross the course of the aqueduct as it passes into the orchard on your left, heading east again and running parallel and about 50 metres to the left of, Route d'Uzès (D3b).

Photograph 9. Waypoint 24

The course of the aqueduct through the fields is only known from distinctive rubble ploughed up by farmers and from shadowy crop marks visible on Google Maps © (Waypoints 25 and 26), although nothing is visible at ground level.

As you approach Argilliers the course of the aqueduct becomes even less well defined, the only clues coming from fortuitous excavations during house building (Waypoints 27 to 32). The assumed course of the aqueduct is parallel to the D3b and about 50 metres on your right.

As you approach a prominent stream known as *le grand Vallat* you will pass the location of Waypoint 31 on the right side of the road, and after a further 100 metres you pass the location of Waypoint 32 on the left side. A close examination of the sides of the roadside ditches may reveal fragments of the channel lining and calcretions from the channel walls but none were visible to the Author or his companions.

After a further 150 metres, just before Chemin de la Grand Combe, the course of the aqueduct swings to the left. Turn left here and follow the road for about 100 metres until the road divides into three by a DFCI sign. Take the track on the right which runs parallel to the course of the aqueduct, which is under the bank on your right. When you reach the end of the track, indicated by two old stone gateposts, make a U turn to the right. Almost immediately on your right you will see a short section of the cement lined left hand wall of the aqueduct **(Waypoint 33 - La Bourache)** before it disappears into a tangle of brambles. Walk past the brambles and you will see larger pieces of the wall together with traces of the vault. After about 50 metres the wall disappears and is replaced by the natural rock face which appears to have been cut back to form the left hand wall of the aqueduct.   Ignoring a more recent ditch, keep to the right and another section of cement lined wall is visible.   The determined aqueducteur can follow the wall into a pit (which has sadly been used to dump rubbish) where a further section of wall is visible. The pit is more easily accessed by returning to Chemin de la Grande Combe, turning left, going 50 metres downhill and climbing down from the roadside.

Return to the stone gateposts and walk eastwards across the field (crops permitting) you are following the course of the aqueduct. When you reach the end of a line of trees you will find yourself between two fields of vines, divided by a ditch and bank, which may conceal the aqueduct. When you reach the road (Chemin de Puits de Mariargues) there is a concrete conduit, the construction of which revealed and then obliterated Waypoint 34. Turn right and proceed about 150 metres down the road until you reach the first row of vines, turn left and head towards the tree line.

If the field after Waypoint 33 contains crops it will be necessary to return to Chemin de la Grande Combe and Route d'Uzès. Turn left and proceed for about 300 metres until you reach Chemin de Puits de Mariargues and turn left. After about 200 metres, at the end of a new area of vines turn right and walk across the field until you reach the tree line.

About 10 metres before your reach the trees you cross the course of the aqueduct, which runs almost parallel to the road. Sadly, it has been recently destroyed by the farmer extending his field, but if you turn right and follow the tree line after about 20 metres you will see a pile of rubble which has come from the destroyed aqueduct. Amongst this rubble are several massive pieces which you can identify as sections of the walls of the aqueduct channel together with the cement lining and thick layers of striated calcretions.

Turn right and follow the bank and then turn left to follow the tree line. The course of the aqueduct is now a few metres on your left and if you look carefully amongst the undergrowth you will see several pieces of the external wall of the channel set into the bank. **(Waypoint 35 - La Coste)**. After about 100 metres the course of the aqueduct turns into the trees but a further section can be found by following the tree line until you reach a large pine tree. Shortly after this tree is an opening into the wooded area. Turn left and pass through an open glade where a 10 metre length of the left hand wall of the aqueduct can be seen in front of you.

The course of the aqueduct continues through the wooded area, but this is largely impenetrable. The next opportunity to re-join the course is where the aqueduct makes a slow 90° bend to the left to run roughly parallel to the D3b (now named Route d'Argilliers) and where it is difficult, but not impossible, to locate.

Continue following the tree line until you almost reach the road and you will find an opening on your left and into the wooded area. Follow the path for about 10 metres and climb up the bank to your left. Several large pieces of the aqueduct (**Waypoint 36**) can be found, notably behind a large slab of rock lying on the bank. This includes a large section of what appears to be the core of the right hand wall, with the dressed stones removed (Photograph 10). If you follow the course of the channel towards the east, you will also find several pits in the ground which may be evidence of the collapse of the aqueduct channel.

Photograph 10. Waypoint 36

6.3 Around Vers-Pont-du-Gard
Map 4 - Waypoints 37 to 50

Distance: ~5 km   Walking Time: ~2 hours

Waypoint	Form	Description
37	VS/NA	20 metre length of calcretion at top of vault. No longer accessible.
38 - La Coste	VS/NA	Short length of calcretion at top of vault (in private garden)
39 - Le Village	VS	Top of vault at edge of road, extends into private garden
40 - Pont du Roc Plan I	VS	Wall with three arches, very overgrown, 20 metres long
41 - Pont due Roc Plan II	VS	Wall with three arches, 45 metres long
47 - Ponceau du Coste Belle	VS/NA	Very overgrown wall and channel 25 metres long, ponceau no longer visible.
49A	VO	Left hand side of channel cut in limestone bedrock
50 - Le Clos des Touillers	VS	60 metre length of the aqueduct with two regards.

The aqueduct approaches the commune of Vers-Pont-du-Gard from the west and loops around the north of the village before travelling southwards. Several minor valleys in this area resulted in the need for sharp changes in direction and the building of several interesting structures. Despite extensive quarrying in the area, and much modern building, a few vestiges are still visible to the west, north and east of Vers including two bridges, a very overgrown culvert, two regards and an extended length of the vault. Housing development in Vers also makes it impossible to follow the course of the aqueduct very closely and some of the vestiges are on private land. As a result the suggested walking route sometimes veers away from the course of the aqueduct, although it does include all of the extant vestiges.

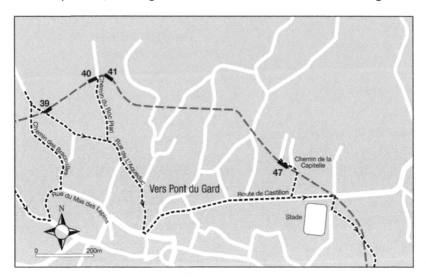

Map 4.   Vers-Pont-du-Gard

Approaching Vers the course of the aqueduct turns sharply to the north to follow the edge of a small but quite prominent valley. It travels up the eastern side of the valley to a point about 200 metres from the road before forming a hairpin and returning down the western side to again run parallel with the road about 20 metres away from it. It is impossible to follow the course of the aqueduct through the dense trees and undergrowth and it is best to stay on the road and head into Vers.

A 2 metre section, comprising the concretions from the top of the vault (**Waypoint 38 - La Coste**) is visible in the garden of the second house along the road and the owner very kindly showed it to me. He may be equally friendly to the occasional aqueducteur.

Enter the village of Vers and turn left into Rue du Mas des Lapins, go past the Domaine de Valsenière on your left and join Chemin des Bracoules. Turn left on to Chemin de Carrière and after about 100 metres the road narrows and you will see, opposite a quarry, a mobile phone tower and the chateau d'eau (water reservoir) on the left. Walk across the front of the building and pick your way through an overgrown area (there is the suggestion of a path, alongside a garden fence). This path had become very overgrown in 2021 but if you proceed with care down the side of the valley and you will come across a sharp drop, which takes you over the top of the vault of the aqueduct as it returns down western edge of the valley (**Waypoint 37**).

Return to Chemin des Carrières and go downhill turning left at the fork after the quarry. Keeping to the left side of the road, after about 100 metres you will see at your feet, projecting into the road from under a wall, a short section of the channel (**Waypoint 39 - Le Village**), complete with calcretions and a suggestion of the vault.

This tiny vestige is overlooked by a stone face, maybe a ghost of the mensor keeping an eye on his handiwork (Photograph 11). Look into the garden behind the wall and you can see the top of the aqueduct which forms the foundation of a boundary wall between two properties before disappearing about 20 metres into the garden.

Photograph 11. Waypoint 39 - Le Village

Continue along Chemin des Carrières for about 250 metres until you reach Chemin du Roc Plan on your left. Take this road for about 200 metres until just before you reach the entrance to the quarry. This is the location of a pair of 'skewed bridges'.

On your left are the abandoned offices of the quarry company, the gates and left hand boundary of which are built on top of the first of the two bridges (**Waypoint 40 - Pont du Roc Plan I**). By scrambling down into the undergrowth to the left hand side of the gate you can see about 20 metres of Roman masonry and, depending on the state of the undergrowth, traces of the three arches revealed by excavation in the 1990s may be visible.

Return to the road, cross to the opposite side and go uphill for about 10 metres where you will find an overgrown path on your right. The course of the aqueduct has changed slightly towards the south at this point, hence the description of the two bridges as 'skewed'. On the right of the path look out for pieces of the left hand wall which eventually leads to a section of channel on top of a massive three arched bridge (**Waypoint 41 - Pont du Roc Plan II** - Photograph 12).

Photograph 12. Waypoint 41- Pont du Roc Plan II

The best view of the bridge is obtained by walking round the edge of the boundary of the property on your right and viewing it from the far side.

Unfortunately, a combination of modern house building and quarrying have destroyed or rendered inaccessible Waypoints 42 to 46. The route to the next visible vestige is to return to Chemin des

Carrières, proceed down Rue de l'Aqueduc, and make your way to Route de Castillon (D192) by way of Rue du Mûrier and Rue du Moulin a Vent. Turn left and walk towards Castillon until you reach Chemin de la Capitelle on your left, just before the Stade Municipale on your right.

Go up Chemin de la Capitelle, round a left hand bend and, just before a sharp right hand bend, turn to face left. You may see a very overgrown piece of wall in front of an abandoned farmhouse, the *Mazet du Marin* (**Waypoint 47 - Ponceau du vallon de Coste Belle**). The extremely overgrown nature of this section, of which about 25 metres exists, means that the two most interesting features of this vestige, a culvert and a slabbed roof, are not currently visible. The use of a large slabs of stone instead of a curved vault is unusual, the only other example being over the water channel on the Pont du Gard. In 2021 permission had been given for the construction of a new house in this location and we can only hope that the presence of this rather unusual part of the aqueduct is respected during the building work.

The course of the aqueduct now begins to bear southwards and is best followed by returning to Route de Castillon and turning right into Chemin du Stade, this being the point at which the aqueduct crosses the road. Excavations in the 1980s showed that the aqueduct passed under the gateway of the first property on your left and diagonally across the plot now occupied by the house and garden (Waypoint 48).

The course of the aqueduct here is again uncertain although excavations in 1996 in Chemin des Charbonnières did locate pieces of it. These suggested that it followed a rather serpentine route although nothing can be seen now as the area is now fully occupied by houses. Follow Chemin du Stade for about 50 metres and turn left into Chemin des Charbonnières. The aqueduct passes under the houses on your left and after about 200 m, at the junction with Chemin du Stade, it passes under the road and continues under the front gardens of the houses on your right.

After a further 100 metres turn right into Chemin du Clos des Touillers and almost immediately on your left you will see a track which is the location of Waypoint 48B. This track is a dead end so you must continue along Chemin du Clos des Touillers for a further 150 metres before turning sharp left into Chemin des Abeilles. After about 100 metres on your left is a cul de sac and a row of new houses. The course of the aqueduct passes under the back gardens of the houses on the right hand side of the road and Waypoint 49 lies beneath the garden of the house nearest to you.

On the opposite side of the road from those houses is an old tree set in a bank. Climb up alongside three and look towards a wooded area beyond, you will see a gap in a second bank about 10 metres from the road. Look carefully and you will see a short length of cut back limestone (**Waypoint 49A**). This vestige is probably evidence for the aqueduct having been placed in a channel cut in the limestone bedrock, of which this is the left hand side. On a personal note, I discovered this 'new' vestige myself in 2021 after the undergrowth had been recently cleared, and I was well chuffed to do so!

Continue through the gap and towards the wooded area, turn left on to the path runs alongside it. After about 20 metres take the path on your right and follow this until it passes through a collapsed section of an old stone wall, turn left on to the path in front of you. The path turns almost immediately to the right but you should make your way through the trees in front of you where you will find the beginning of the next vestige (**Waypoint 50 - Le Clos des Touillers**). This section of the aqueduct is about 60 metres long and, once again, it provides the base of a more recent dry stone wall. The first view is of a ruined regard followed by an extended length of the top of the vault running roughly parallel with the path and partly concealed by trees.

Photograph 13. Waypoint 50 - Regard at Le Clos des Touillers

After about 40 metres a gap in the trees reveals a section where a slot has been cut into the calcretions presumably by an archaeologist investigating the flow rate history in the aqueduct. About 5 metres further along the path you will find a second more complete regard located at a change of direction of the aqueduct (Photograph 13).

An interesting feature of this section of the aqueduct is that the calcretions cover the underside of the vault as well as the walls which suggests that the channel ran completely full of water for an extended period.

Continue along the path and bear left to climb over the aqueduct near to a large oak tree. Continue on this path and turn right when you reach the junction with another path. The course of the aqueduct is on your right, sometimes very close to this path. After about 50 metres there is a break in the undergrowth and you can see the top of the channel and a steep drop on its right hand side. Continue for another 5 metres and turn right crossing a line of stones which are the remains of the left hand wall of the aqueduct. Follow this path for about 100 metres and turn left at the end on to a stony track. At the top of the rise you will see the aqueduct emerging from the bank on your left. The channel crosses the path with the distinctive 'tramline' form with both walls and striated calcretions (Photograph 14).

Photograph 14.   Waypoint 50

6.4 Vers-Pont-du-Gard to the Pont du Gard
Map 5 - Waypoints 51 to 58

Distance: ~2 km   **Walking Time: ~1½ hours**

Waypoint	Form	Description
51 - Pont à arcades de la Lône	VS	Rubble covered bank leads to 400 metres of wall and arcade
52 - Pont de Font Ménestière	VS	Massive foundations of several pillars on each side of road
53 - Pont à arcades de Pont Roupt	VS	300 metres of wall and arcade
54 - Martian	VS	Short piece of wall and 10 metre length of calcretion
55 - Pont à arcades de Valive	VS	100 metres of wall and arcade, ends with 45°bend to left
56 - Bassin régulateur	VS?	Stones projecting above ground
57 - Pont du Gard	VS	400 metre long three tier bridge
58	VS	Aqueduct disappears into hillside

The remains of the aqueduct between Vers and the Pont du Gard constitute one of the most interesting but often ignored sections of the entire aqueduct. Over this stretch the aqueduct had to cross a series of small depressions as the land begins to fall away towards the valley of the Gardon. This left the mensor with no option but to build several extended stretches of walls and arcades to elevate the channel and preserve the limited fall. It was also necessary to build a massive bridge over Col de la Ratade.

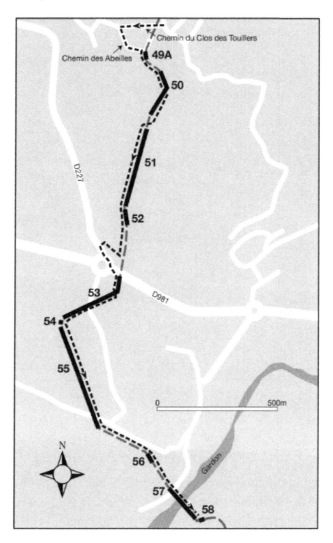

Map 5.   Vers-Pont-du-Gard to the Pont du Gard

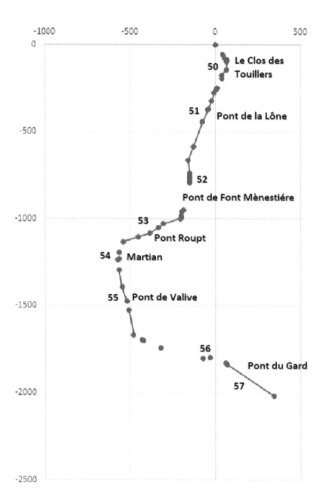

Figure 5. Visible vestiges Waypoints 50 to 57 (Scale in m)

After crossing the final piece of Waypoint 50 continue climbing to the top of the rise and immediately in front of you is an overgrown bank of rubble, which is located on top of the aqueduct. Following the aqueduct is now the easiest that it has been since you left Uzès and you will benefit from taking your time and enjoying a wide range of features along this section (**Waypoint 51 - Pont à arcades de la Lône**).

This section has a total length of about 600 metres of which 400 metres show obvious stonework. This includes an 80 metre length of wall followed by the Pont de la Lône, which comprises a series of arches in various states of repair. Of particular interest are the massive lumps of calcretion which resulted from water leakage over an extended period, either accidental or deliberate, the latter thought to be a result of farmers diverting water for crop irrigation. The first calcretion is visible shortly after the wall emerges from the stony bank and, as well as being huge, it includes evidence that some kind of wooden structure was used, possibly to create an illicit run-off channel. At many points along this section, you will also see examples of 'curtain' calcretions, where water leaking from the channel has run down the external sides of the supporting walls and deposited calcium salts on them.

Once you reach the arched section (Photograph 15), one obvious feature is that many of the arches have been filled in after their original construction. This may have been done to prevent sagging of the channel due to the considerable weight of water it contained, combined with the weight of the calcretions. Also visible are several steps taken to give the supporting walls and arcade lateral stability using buttresses on both sides and additional foundations. Archaeologists have found evidence of earthquake damage to the aqueduct in this section and this, or poor foundations, may be the reason for the reinforcement.

It is not obvious whether the elevated channel had a vaulted roof or was slabbed, as was the case in the Le Claux de Melet (Waypoint 44) and, more obviously, at the Pont du Gard. Only a single fragment of the channel itself is visible in this section and it suggests that the more conventional vaulted roof was used.

Photograph 15. Waypoint 51 - Pont de la Lône

A particular interesting feature is to be found in some of the filled in arches where a chamber has been created under the arch and a small arched entrance constructed to allow access. Although these access ways appear Roman in their construction local rumours say that the Wehrmacht used the arches of the Pont de la Lône to store ammunition during the Second World War, but others say that they were used for a similar purpose by the French Resistance.

As you follow the Pont de la Lône southwards you are gradually climbing uphill and the height of the arcade progressively reduces, before eventually disappearing. Almost immediately afterwards the ground begins to fall away steeply into Col de la Ratade, a deep steep sided valley now occupied by a disused railway line and the D981. Following the path downhill you pass on your left the massive foundations of the Pont de Font Mènestiére (**Waypoint 52 - Pont à deux étages de Font Mènestiére**).

This bridge is now totally destroyed apart from these foundations, which are visible of both sides of the valley, but it must have been a magnificent sight being approximately 250 metres long and up to 20 metres high. How it actually appeared is anybody's guess but it was likely a two tier structure, like the similarly sized (and also destroyed) bridge in Combe Roussière.

The stonework of the bridge was likely robbed at some stage, the final insult being the dynamiting of some of its foundations on the northern side during the construction of the now defunct Remoulins/Alès railway line during the 19th century. An interesting feature of the pairs of foundation stones is the presence of dovetailed mortices which were used to lock the stones together using either wooden or metal tenons (Photograph 16).

Turn right at the edge of the railway cutting and proceed down the hill to the Route du Misserand (D227). Turn left at the bottom, cross the roundabout on the D981, go through the gate in front of you and turn left again. Before you do, glance back at the valley and imagine the bridge that crossed it, with the water channel at the same height as the highest of the trees on either side. After about 50 metres climb the steep set of steps on your right and walk pass the foundations of the southern pillars of the bridge.

Photograph 16. Waypoint 52 - Pont de Font Mènestiére

At the top of the hill, the aqueduct returns to the arcade form and turns through 45^0 to the southwest. There now follows another extended arcade (Photograph 17) which includes a few fragments of the original channel, this section being known as the Pont Roupt or 'ruptured bridge' (**Waypoint 53 - Pont à arcades de Pont Roupt**).

After about 200 metres and two further bends the wall disappears as the land rises and the aqueduct goes underground to pass around and partly through the col de Martian where the aqueduct makes a 90^0 turn to the south. On the right of the path you will see where a shallow excavation has revealed the left hand wall of the channel and a little further along there is a line of calcretions projecting out of the ground for a distance of about 10 metres (**Waypoint 54 - Martian**).

There now follows another extended combination of wall and arcade, the latter being known as the Pont du Valive (**Waypoint 55 - Pont à arcades de Valive** - Photograph 18).

Photograph 17. Waypoint 53 - Pont Roupt

After about 200 metres the land rises again and the aqueduct disappears, but the path continues along the course of the aqueduct, as indicated by the yellow arrows on the trees. Shortly after the end of the Pont de Valive the course of the aqueduct makes a 45° turn to the southeast and if you take the lower path of the two through a stand of trees and look carefully on the ground to your right at and you may find a short length of dressed stones on this new alignment. A little further along the path a line of dressed stones is visible near to what appears to be a milestone.

Photograph 18. Waypoint 55 - Pont de Valive

The land now begins to fall into the gorge of the Gardon. Look out for the rather desultory remains of a regulator basin (**Waypoint 56 - Bassin Régulateur**) excavated in 1988 but subsequently reburied. The purpose of this regulator was to control the quantity of water passing over the Pont du Gard by diverting some of the flow into the Gardon and preventing overflowing of the channel on the bridge. Excavations revealed a similar structure to that seen in Uzès (Waypoint 2A) but sadly all that remains visible here now are a few stones projecting out of the ground. With a little imagination a V-notch can be seen on the largest of the stones which may be part of the overflow mechanism.

The land now falls more steeply, the stonework that made up the arcade that was here having been robbed completely (allegedly by

Monks in the 15th century) leaving the next vestige (**Waypoint 57-Pont du Gard)** rather isolated at its north end. All that remains of the northern arcade is the core of a single missing pillar, robbed of its massive covering stones. In front of you now is the jewel in the crown that is the Nîmes aqueduct.

The Pont du Gard (Photograph 19) is the highest Roman aqueduct bridge still in existence, its size being enhanced by its location; isolated in the middle of the garrigue. Indeed, were it not for its UNESCO World Heritage status and the flocks of tourists bussed in to see it every day, particularly during the summer months, it would be difficult to find!

Photograph 19. Waypoint 57 - Pont du Gard

The bridge is the most spectacular vestige of the entire aqueduct, indeed many think that it is *the* aqueduct rather than a relatively small part of it. I recommend that you visit the Pont du Gard early in the morning or late in the evening. That way you will have it to yourself and will get the full value from seeing it in isolation in the landscape, as it was when it was part of the functioning aqueduct.

The bridge has three tiers of arches with the lowest row having 6 arches with a height of 22 m; the middle row having 11 arches with a height of 20 m; and the upper row, which comprises the water channel itself, having 35 (there were originally 47) arches with a height of 7 metres. The width of the bridge varies from 9 metres at the bottom to 3 metres at the top. After extensive stone robbing of the northern end the bridge now has an overall length of 274 metres (of an original length of over 400 metres) and a maximum height of almost 50 metres.

The Pont du Gard was not designed for traffic rather as a support for the aqueduct channel. However, in the early 18th century the pillars of the second tier were partly cut away to allow mules to cross the Gardon. This put the whole structure at risk of collapse and in 1747 the road bridge, constructed by Pitot, was opened and the damage to the second tier pillars repaired. Much of the material for the road bridge was taken from the north end of the Pont du Gard, the remainder being from the same quarries used by the Romans.

At the southern end of the bridge, the striated patterns in the massive calcretion deposits are clearly visible on both sides of the channel as it turns sharply to the left and disappears into the opposite bank **(Waypoint 58)**. In front of you is the tunnel created as part of the ill-fated Canal de Pouzin but, as we are going with the Roman flow, you should turn left and follow the pathway; the 'real' aqueduct is buried beneath the trees on your right.

6.5 Through the Bois de Remoulins

Map 6 - Waypoints 59 to 100

Distance: ~9 km   Walking Time: ~5 hours

Waypoint	Form	Description
59	VS	Short length of dressed stones
60	VS	30 metres of right hand wall and concretions
61	VS	Outer wall with brickwork and channel behind
62 - Valley 1, Pont de Valmale	VS	Broken arch with channel on both sides, 70 metres total
63	VS	Excavated channel followed by dressed stone
64	VS	Bend, aligned stone and 35 metre section of outer wall
65 - Valley 2	VO	Depression at bend
66	VS	Excavated channel
67	VS	30 metre length of excavated channel
68 - Valley 3, Pont de la Combe Roussière	VS	Two massive abutments followed by 35 metres of channel
69	VS	Channel disappears into hillside
70 - Valley 4	VS	Partly excavated channel

Waypoint	Form	Description
71	VS	Partly excavated channel
72	VS	Several pieces of left hand wall, total 120 metres
73 - Valley 5, Pont de la Sartanette	VS	Intact arch with channel before and after, 70 metres in total
74	VS	Excavated channel (2 pieces) and left hand wall, total 10 metres
75	VS	20 metre section of left hand wall
76	VS	15 metre section of left hand wall followed by U-section in limestone with overflow notch and ~80 metre section of supporting wall
77	VS	Excavated 60° bend
79 - Valley 6, the Little Bridge	VS	40 metres of channel, over culvert
Approach to 85	VS	20 metre length of top of right hand wall in undergrowth
85 - Valley 7, Pont de la Combe Joseph	VS	140 metre section of channel over intact bridge.
86	VS	10 metre length of wall
90	VS	Short length of channel approaching bridge abutment
91 - Valley 8, Pont de la Combe Pradier	VS	Damaged but intact bridge
92	VS	Several extended lengths of right hand wall with traces of left hand wall and base of channel

Waypoint	Form	Description
93	VS	Cut back limestone face with some dressed stone and base of channel
94	VS	Short length of left hand wall
95- Valley 9	VS	Curved section of right hand wall, total ~15 metres
96 - Valley 10, Pont de la Combe de Gilles	VS	Intact bridge and walls, total ~25 metres
99 - Valley 11	VS	Buttressed curved wall and several pieces of channel, total ~35 metres
100 - Chemin des Arbousiers	VS	Short length of right hand wall

Having left the Pont du Gard, hopefully amazed by the skill and ingenuity of the builders, you come across what was possibly a much greater achievement by those same builders. The densely wooded and valleyed area between the Gardon and Saint Bonnet du Gard, now known as the Bois de Remoulins, will have provided a serious challenge during the construction of this section of the aqueduct. If we could strip away the trees and undergrowth from this area it would expose a steep hillside rutted with several deep valleys that were cut into the limestone over the aeons by the rainwater that periodically pours off the hillside and into the Gardon. The challenge to the mensor, who was faced with the task of planning a route through this area, covered with what was probably dense virgin woodland, was considerable. Then the construction gangs who had to fulfil his plans would have been similarly challenged when digging trenches in the limestone and building the supporting walls and bridges.

For much of this piece of the aqueduct the channel was built using an L-section, with the right hand side formed by cut back limestone bedrock. In some places both the external (left hand) wall, occasionally faced with dressed stones, and the right hand wall are visible. In other places only the chiselled face of the limestone remains. Occasionally it was necessary to cut trenches in the limestone, sometimes several metres deep, the aqueduct channel being constructed within these trenches.

After its construction the aqueduct was relatively easily accessed and after it was abandoned it became a ready supply of dressed stones to anybody with a cart. As a result, particular in the case of the magnificent bridge in Combe Roussière, many of the stones that made up the bridges and the exterior walls of the aqueduct, together with the massive layers of calcretion, were extensively robbed in the Middle Ages and used to build churches and houses in Remoulins and Saint-Bonnet-du-Gard.

In total there are 11 valleys of differing severity (not including the Gardon gorge) and a number of more minor and side valleys. This resulted in a serpentine route (Figure 6) and the construction of 7 bridges or ponceaux (culverts) of assorted designs and sizes.

The Bois de Remoulins provides the most difficult but rewarding piece of the aqueduct for both the casual and the determined aqueducteur. In total there are at least 30 visible vestiges (Figure 7) which between them capture every feature of the aqueduct. There are undoubtedly several more, but these lie in the impenetrable undergrowth that characterises the area.

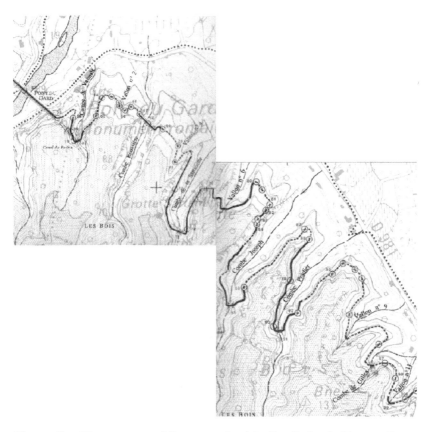

Figure 6. The course of the aqueduct in the Bois de Remoulins

Many of the vestiges listed above are accessible by a well-made path that initially follows the course of the aqueduct, or by others that avoid the more overgrown areas. However, be warned, accessing some of those vestiges will require a determined approach to defeating the terrain. Good walking boots, robust clothing and walking poles are recommended, I have fallen into the spiny undergrowth on more than one occasion!

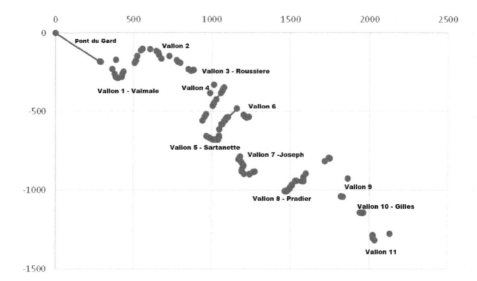

Figure 7. Visible vestiges in the Bois de Remoulins (Scale in m)

Hacking through the Bois de Remoulins gives one a real feeling of exploration and finding some of the vestiges will give you a real sense of discovery. But one should never lose sight of the fact that 2,000 years ago the virgin woods were even more impenetrable than they are today and that the paths that make it relatively easy to follow so much of the aqueduct's twists and turns did not exist. Add to this the fact that you are simply walking the course of the aqueduct, the Romans were actually building it.

As mentioned above, the designers of the Canal de Pouzin planned to use the Pont du Gard to carry water over the Gardon valley and to generally follow the aqueduct through the Bois de Remoulins. Fortunately, they decided to bypass most of the valleys and drive tunnels through the interfluves, the first of which is visible at the southern end of the Pont du Gard. This resulted in the destruction of

84

only relatively small pieces of the aqueduct, unlike the more wholesale vandalism that occurred to east of Nîmes.

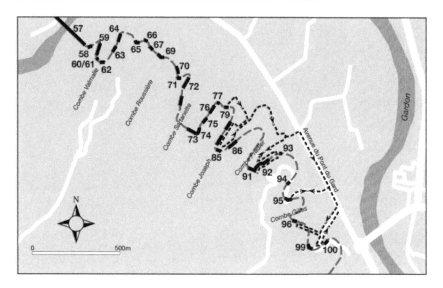

Map 6.   The Bois de Remoulins

As you leave the Pont du Gard, ignore the Pouzin Tunnel in front of you (maybe shaking your head at its folly) and follow the path to your left.   The path runs approximately alongside the course of the aqueduct which can be seen immediately on your right as a short length of excavated channel disappearing into the hillside (**Waypoint 58 -** Photograph 20).

Valley 1 – Combe de Valmale

Follow the path along the edge of the valley, the course of the aqueduct remains on your right close to the path as witnessed by an excavated pit and a 10 metre length of cut back limestone. After the paths turns sharply to the right there is a section of the right hand

85

wall of the channel with traces of the vault together with significant pieces of calcretion (**Waypoint 59**).

Photograph 20. Waypoint 58 and the Pouzin Tunnel

Immediately before the exit of the Pouzin Tunnel there is a large piece of the right hand wall of the channel again coated with a thick layer of calcretion. The tunnel destroyed a section of the aqueduct here and all that now remains is approximately 100 metres of cut back limestone (**Waypoint 60**).

Towards the end of this section, the path drops off to the left but ahead of you on your right is a 90° bend (**Waypoint 61**) which includes both sides of the channel and some of the original dressed stonework on the external face of the left hand wall. This short section (Photograph 21) gives you an idea how the external faces of the above ground sections of the aqueduct would have looked when it was built and before the facing stones were robbed. It is so typically Roman, making a purely functional construction look beautiful.

Photograph 21. Waypoint 61

Here again the Canal de Pouzin was cut through the aqueduct and a further piece of the latter is visible on the left of the gap left by the former. Thankfully, as the aqueduct turned to the left the canal continued straight on disappearing into the garrigue on your right,.

The aqueduct continues to curve to the left until it reaches **Waypoint 62 - Pont de Valmale**. The bridge originally had a single arch which spanned about 3 metres although only the abutments now remain (Photograph 22).

Photograph 22. Waypoint 62 - Pont de Valmale

Climbing down to look at the underside of the heavily restored bridge reveals some of the original beautiful Roman masonry, particularly in the lower courses. Note also the buttressing of the bridge which appears to have been added after the bridge was built, (the buttress walls are not bonded to the main walls of the bridge), presumably to provide additional lateral stability.

Climb up the opposite side of the bridge and you will see a short length of supporting wall after which the aqueduct makes a 45° turn to the left. The path continues to follow the course of the aqueduct which is on your right hand side. Keep looking down and you will see the occasional line of dressed stone from the outside face of the left hand wall (including **Waypoint 63**) together with sections of the right hand wall set into the bank. After about 200 metres there is a short, excavated section of the whole channel including a 90⁰ bend (**Waypoint 64**).

The path now crosses a more substantial track and if you keep to the right hand side of the path you are walking inside the channel of the aqueduct. There now follows a 35 metre length of the left hand wall, two slight bends to the right, and an excavated section, as the course of the aqueduct turns into Valley 2 (**Waypoint 65**).

Valley 2

Valley 2 is not very prominent and it only resulted in a small deviation in the course of the aqueduct, without any need for a bridge or a culvert. As you approach the valley you will observe more lines of dressed stone on the right hand edge of the path which then makes a 90⁰ turn to the left to exit the valley. Shortly after the turn is a short length of excavated channel (**Waypoint 66**).

Valley 3 – Combe Roussière

Whilst Valley 2 is probably the lesser of the eleven valleys in the Bois de Remoulins, Valley 3 is definitely the most prominent. As you approach the edge of the valley you will see more evidence for cutting back of the limestone bedrock on the right hand side of the path and immediately before the northern abutment of the bridge (Photograph 23) there is an excavated section of the channel approximately 25 metres long and including a 45⁰ bend. The aqueduct channel is here well below ground level and its partial blockage by calcretion is very obvious.

The bridge that was built to cross Valley 3 would have been a very impressive sight, spanning over 100 metres and rising up to 40 metres above the valley floor. However, the convenience of its location led to its use as a quarry in the Middle Ages which virtually destroyed the entire structure. That being said, the two massive abutments (**Waypoints 67 and 68 - Pont à 2 étages de la Combe Roussière**) that survive are breath taking in their own right and at least partly convey the grand scale of the bridge.

Photograph 23. Waypoint 68 - Pont de la Combe Roussière

The best impression of the missing bridge can be obtained by walking (carefully!) to the edge of the northern abutment and looking across to its southern counterpart. This allows you to imagine how the bridge might have looked before the stone robbers destroyed it.

As you climb down into the valley look back at the well preserved dressed facing stones on the face of the northern abutment, this was indeed a mighty structure. The size of the remnants of the foundations of the missing pillars indicate that the bridge had two levels, with at least three massive arches on the lower tier and, assuming similar dimensions as those of the Pont du Gard, between ten and twelve arches supporting the water channel on the upper tier.

Scrambling up the opposite side of the valley you will see a scatter of dressed and shaped stones and the cores of the bases of two of the pillars, again the immensity of the bridge is very apparent. There is a question as to why the mensor chose to build such a massive bridge here rather than take the course of the aqueduct further up the valley where it is narrower and where it may only have required a smaller single arched bridge such as those at Valmale or Sartanette. However, as well as being deep Combe Roussière also has very steep sides which could have made it very difficult to build the aqueduct along its edges.

After the southern abutment there is approximately 35 metres of channel visible, including a sharp 90° bend to the left and a longer sweeping bend to the right. Once again the outer surfaces of the walls being faced with delicately curved dressed stones.

Continue to follow the path, the aqueduct is again on your right. Shortly after the bridge there is a deep excavation where both walls of the channel and a small piece of the vault are visible (**Waypoint**

69). After a further 200 metres the path and the course of the aqueduct make a 90° right turn to follow the edge of Valley 4, a short section of the left hand wall is visible here.

Valley 4

Valley 4 is relatively minor undulation in the landscape but one which required a deviation of about 60 metres in the course of the aqueduct. Both the path and the aqueduct make a sharp left hand turn at a point indicated by an excavated pit and where a small section of the outer face of the left hand wall is visible (**Waypoint 70 - Vallon No. 4**). This is followed by two further pieces of the left hand wall (**Waypoint 71**) behind which is a 2 metre high area where the limestone has been cut back to form the right hand wall. The path now turns right to run along the edge of Valley 5.

Valley 5 – Combe de la Sartanette

The aqueduct now follows the northern side of Valley 5 where there are several visible vestiges (**Waypoint 72**) totalling about 200 metres, generally located only a metre or two from the right hand side of the path. This includes extensive pieces of the left hand wall and evidence for the removal of the limestone rock face. In places the limestone bedrock has been excavated to form a 2 metre wide trench inside which the aqueduct was constructed. At one point it is possible to enter the trench through what appears to be a man-made opening. This slot may have been created to allow dirty surface water to drain from the trench to prevent it from entering the aqueduct channel and contaminating the clean spring water. This is further witnessed by a large lump of calcretion at the bottom of the slot.

There now follows about 100 metres of continuous left hand wall often partly concealed by dense undergrowth. This includes a section nearly 2 metres high where both walls of the aqueduct are still present. The obvious presence of the left hand wall, often faced with dressed stone, suggests that the channel is relative intact behind the wall, albeit filled with rubble and many centuries worth of earth and leaf mould.

When you reach the bridge (**Waypoint 73 - Pont de la Sartanette** - Photograph 24), two things are worthy of note; the depth of the channel before and over the bridge and the degree of obstruction caused by calcretion. The latter caused the original 1.2 metre wide channel to be reduced to as little as 0.3 metres at the bottom.

Photograph 24. Waypoint 73 - Pont de la Sartanette

The bridge itself has been extensively but sympathetically restored with much of the original stonework still visible, together with a secondary wall which provided additional reinforcement. Walking through the channel on the north side of the bridge illustrates how the above ground sections of the aqueduct channel were constructed with two massive external walls faced on the outside with dressed stone and lined on the inside with waterproof cement.

After the bridge, the aqueduct makes a sharp bend to the left (**Waypoint 74**) where striations in the calcretion are clearly visible. The path continues to follow the course of the aqueduct for about 100 metres and a number of sunken areas and pieces of the left hand wall are visible.

After about 200 metres resist the temptation to turn right and climb uphill but rather follow the less obvious path in front of you and into a partially overgrown area. In the summer of 2021 this path was challenging but certainly not impenetrable and it leads to several pieces of the aqueduct as it skirts the southern side of the valley. After about 30 metres the aqueduct is visible on the left hand side of the path, shortly after which a short section of the top of the right hand wall is visible on the right side of the path. After a further 50 metres, just past a large rock, the left hand wall reappears on the right hand side of the path (**Waypoint 75**). This 20 metre length shows how the dressed stones that made up the outer surface of the channel have been robbed exposing the core and, in some places, the outer face of the cement lining of the channel.

After a short break the left hand wall reappears together with a length of the cut back limestone (**Waypoint 76**). About 30 metres of both walls of the aqueduct are visible, together with the left wall of the trench that was cut in the limestone to accommodate the aqueduct. Also visible is another slot cut in the left hand wall of the trench, again possibly created to allow rainwater to drain from the trench.

The aqueduct now curves to the right and you have to climb on top of the supporting wall by use of the projecting core stones. On your left now is a 2 metre drop which is the left hand face of this supporting wall. This can be examined by turning left through a gap in the trees and scrambling down the bank. The aqueduct then curves to the left and, after a total of about 100 metres, it turns sharply to the right (**Waypoint 77**). This turn has been fully excavated and this shows how deep underground the aqueduct was at this point.

Valley 6 – The 'Little Bridge'

After leaving Waypoint 77 climb in and out of an excavated pit (although no obvious remains of the aqueduct are visible) and follow the path to the left. The path slopes downwards and after about 100 metres on your right you will see the channel in the form of an excavated right hand bend which leads to the next bridge. You will see where a piece of the calcretion has been cut out, presumably to provide information regarding the rate of accumulation over time and allow the water flow history of the aqueduct to be estimated. The striations in the freshly cut surface of the deposited material are particularly obvious here.

The 'Little Bridge' (**Waypoint 79 - Ponceau du vallon No. 6**) is not so much a bridge as a simple culvert (or *ponceau*) which allowed water running down the valley to pass under the aqueduct channel (Photograph 25). However, the lack of a more traditional arch is more than made up by the impressive construction of the culvert which is made from huge slabs of rock (Photograph 26). It is well worth spending some time examining the 'Little Bridge' as it has many features of interest on both sides of the bridge and within the aqueduct channel itself.

Photograph 25. Waypoint 79 - The Little Bridge

Immediately after the bridge the aqueduct makes a 45^0 bend to the left before disappearing into dense undergrowth. On the outer face of the left hand wall there are some beautifully shaped stones which again give an idea of how the aqueduct would have looked in Roman times.

Photograph 26. Waypoint 79 - Culvert under the Little Bridge

It is currently impossible to follow the course of the aqueduct out of Valley 6 and into Valley 7 due to the density of the undergrowth. The route now is to follow the path that runs down the valley until you reach a path crossing at right angles, turn right and climb out of the valley. The course of the aqueduct crosses the interfluve between the two valleys and is about 100 metres to your right. The author has searched for Waypoints 80 and 81 in this area without success.

After about 200 metres you will drop into Valley 7, Combe Joseph, turn right and follow the path uphill.

Valley 7 – Combe Joseph

The path is an obvious stream bed as evidenced by the deep gouge cut in the ground by what must be large flows of water draining from the garrigue when storms flood the area. After about 400 metres, by a small pile of rocks, take the path to the right and climb out of the valley. After 100 metres next to a second pile of rocks turn right up a small path into the wooded area. About 10 meters up this path, on the left you will see the top of the right hand wall of the aqueduct which continues into the undergrowth. Go back down the path, turn right and continue along the main path. After about 20 metres the wall is visible again on your right as the path crosses the course of the aqueduct.

As you continue along the path you are now walking on top of the channel with a distinct section of the left hand wall on your left and a considerable drop into the overgrown area. At the end of this section a short piece of the right hand wall is also visible. Two slight bends to the left are followed by a 90° bend to the left and the bridge (**Waypoint 85 - Pont de la Combe Joseph**).

This bridge (Photograph 27) has a 'full set' of features including pieces of both walls, the waterproof cement lining and significant calcretions. There is also possible evidence of the red maltha where the calcretions have come away from the cement lining. The single arch of the bridge is damaged but intact and has significant reinforcement on all four flanks and, despite much of the external stonework having been robbed to expose the rough stones of the core, there is still a good quantity of dressed Roman stone visible.

The bridge is followed by a 60° turn to the left and a deep section of channel. Following the path beyond reveals a short length of the right hand wall (**Waypoint 86**). The length of visible aqueduct in the vicinity of the bridge totals about 160 metres.

Photograph 27. Waypoint 85 - Pont de la Combe Joseph

Once again it is currently impossible to follow the course of the aqueduct any further due to dense undergrowth and you should return to the bridge walk to the bottom of Combe Joseph.

Valley 8 – Combe Pradier

Turn right at the bottom of Combe Joseph and follow the path which runs behind the fence of the apartments. The course of the aqueduct is about 50 metres on your right, lost in the garrigue. As you drop into the next valley take the path to the right which again is an obvious stream bed.

After a few hundred metres the path divides, the left fork leading to **Waypoint 91 - Pont de la Combe Pradier**. The bridge originally had a single arch which was subsequently filled in and a culvert formed with large stones (Photograph 28), the structure of which is best observed by returning to the fork in the path and climbing up the stream bed. The bridge has been separated from its northern abutment by a path but if you go through the gap and turn right you will see where the bridge abutment has been buttressed by dressed stone, giving a total width of about 4 metres at ground level.

Climb up on to the wall and you will see traces of the channel, including the concrete base. If you walk a short distance upstream you will find a short length of the channel partially excavated to expose both walls (**Waypoint 90**).

Go back to the fork and take the path on your left, after about 10 metres and on your right is a massive, dressed stone with a mortice t, which must have fallen from the bridge at some point.

Return to the bridge and climb up on to it. After the bridge the aqueduct makes a turn to the left and disappears but if you continue along the path and the aqueduct reappears at your feet and you will find an extended section of the right hand wall. After about 20 metres the wall disappears behind a small clump of trees. Skirt round the left of these trees and there now follows a significant length of the right hand wall, about 100 metres long, together with fragments of the left hand wall, the base of the channel, and pieces of massive calcretion.

Photograph 28. Waypoint 91 - Pont de la Combe Pradier

If you look across the valley, at the same level as where you are standing, you will see evidence of Waypoint 89 in the form of a cut back vertical surface on the bare limestone.

After a short break in the wall there is an excavated section of the channel with two 45° left turns, this deviation in the course of the aqueduct was made necessary by a small side valley. There may well be a culvert under this bend but it is not apparent although the left hand wall is seriously reinforced by a well-built buttress possibly to reinforce the aqueduct against the pressure of water flowing down the valley. Shortly after the bend there is a 20 metre length of the right hand wall (**Waypoint 92** - Photograph 29).

Photograph 29. Waypoint 92

The aqueduct now disappears but the path continues, it being located just below the course of the aqueduct. This is not an easy route to follow although in 2021 somebody had kindly marked it by tying strips of blue and white material to the trees, and some of the rocks have been marked with blue paint. If you are feeling adventurous you can follow this path for about 150 metres and, just before you reach a deep side valley, you will find your reward: **Waypoint 93**. This vestige (Photograph 30) is located above the path on the right hand side of the path and comprises a curved piece of cut back rock face together with several dressed stones and a piece of the base of the channel.

Photograph 30. Waypoint 93

You are now almost at the point where the aqueduct makes a 90^0 turn to the right and over the interfluve into Valley 9. It is just possible to follow the path, still marked by strips of material and painted rocks, but I have not found any further vestiges here. Your best route however is to return to the bridge and retrace your steps down the valley. When you reach the bottom you should turn right and follow the path down to the D981 and turn right again.

Valley 9

Follow the D981 for a few hundred metres and take the track on the right signed DFCI B53 with directions to Saint Bonnet and Le Sablas. After about 200 metres the track bends to the right but if you carry straight on up a path at the apex of the bend you will find a 20 metre section of the right hand wall hidden in the trees (**Waypoint 94 - Vallon No. 9**).

Once again it is impossible to follow the aqueduct into the next valley and the only option is to return to the D981, turn right and after 200 metres turn right again into Chemin des Arbousiers.

Valley 10 – Combe de Gilles

The bridge at Combe de Gilles is reputed to be difficult to find. It certainly is a challenge but it is worth the effort. Follow Chemin des Arbousiers, which lies in the bottom of Valley 11, for about 200 metres and you will see a sharp bend to the left ahead of you. About 10 meters before this bend, you will notice an opening in the trees on your right and a small path which climbs steeply out of Valley 11. At the summit of the path, the onward route is indicated by a series of small cairns. Follow them first to the right and then, with the route tending to the left and straightening as you drop into Valley 10, you will find hidden in the trees; **Waypoint 96 - Pont de la Combe de Gilles**.

The remains comprise about 20 metres of wall incorporating a single arched bridge, which has been partly blocked, possibly to prevent its collapse, leaving a much smaller ponceau which is framed by a semi-circular arch made from beautifully dressed and shaped stones, many of which are still in place (Photograph 31).

Photograph 31. Waypoint 96 - Pont de la Combe de Gilles

This is another of the Author's favourite vestiges, the design of the bridge itself is exquisite and this is enhanced by the isolation of its location. In the spring it is a wonderful place for a picnic, being surrounded by so many wildflowers including several species of wild orchid.

Valley 11

The structure in Valley 11 cannot be found by following the course of the aqueduct from Valley 10 but by returning to Chemin des Arbousiers. Turn right and continue up the hill for about 10 metres to the apex of the sharp bend where a steep path through the trees leads to **Waypoint 99 - Vallon No. 11**).

The vestige (Photograph 32) is a 35 metre curved section of the aqueduct comprising the right hand wall together with substantial pieces of the left hand wall and some heavy buttressing of the whole structure. There does not appear to be any penetration of the supporting wall to allow for the passage of water running off the garrigue although the wall is strongly reinforced by brick-built buttresses and individual large rocks placed against its downhill face.

Photograph 32. Waypoint 99 - Vallon No. 11

A further vestige of the aqueduct can be found in Valley 11 by returning to Chemin des Arbousiers and proceeding about 20 meters uphill where a 6 metre length of lined right hand channel wall

(**Waypoint 100 - Chemin des Arbousiers**) can be seen in the bank on the right hand side of the road, below the modern water reservoir.

It is known that the course of the aqueduct curves around the end of the southern edge of Valley 11, but all traces of this piece were destroyed when the modern water tower was constructed, an interesting irony.

6.6 Saint Bonnet du Gard to Sernhac

Map 7 - Waypoints 101 to 117

Distance: ~9 km   Walking Time: 4 hours

Waypoint	Form	Description
103 Chemin de Sablas	VS	Channel crosses footpath, 'tramlines' visible
104A	VS	10 metre length of right hand wall with cement lining, in trench dug for Canal de Pouzin.
111	VS	Channel cut in bedrock, base of aqueduct and some dressed stonework
112	VS	Bedrock cut back to form right hand wall
113 Tunnel de la Perrotte	VS	Tunnel with regards and stonework
115 Tunnel des Cantarelles	VS	Tunnel with regards and stonework
117 Tunnel de Sernhac village	VS	Regard

After being spoiled and challenged by the plethora of vestiges in the valleys of the Bois de Remoulins the next few kilometres may be considered a disappointment due to the lack of visible vestiges. This is however at least partly compensated by a much gentler walk through typically Gardois scenery and the interesting village of Saint-Bonnet-du-Gard. Notwithstanding the lack of visible stonework the aqueduct has left an impression on the landscape, in the form of the field boundaries and tracks that witness its course. There is also the presence of the excavations made for the Canal de Pouzin which, in this area, follows the course of the aqueduct very closely.

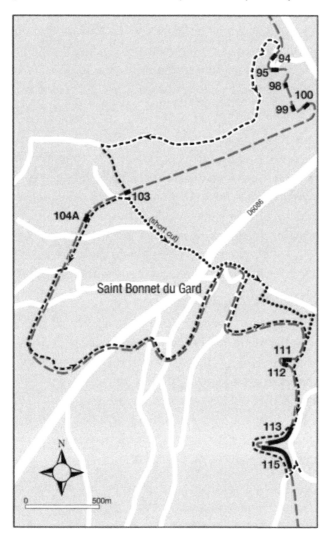

Map 7.   Saint-Bonnet-du-Gard to Sernhac

After the aqueduct leaves the Bois de Remoulins its course traces a huge lazy S through the commune of Saint Bonnet. This route is defined by the local geography and a need to avoid the channel dropping too steeply from the flanks of the Bois de Remoulins and into the valley in which Saint Bonnet is now located. In addition, two significant hills, Marduel and Ferraud, provide formidable obstacles and the aqueduct had to pass between them before heading south towards Sernhac.

At first sight this course appears strange as what seems a more logical and direct route would cut out at least one loop of the S. However, such a route would have resulted in the need for a bridge about 300 metres long and up to 30 metres high. The mensor maybe decided that the benefits of avoiding the construction of such a massive structure made his choice of a longer and more serpentine route more optimal. No matter how strange the route appears it had sufficient logic for it also to be adopted as the route for the Canal de Pouzin 1800 years later.

There is no easy way to closely follow the course of the aqueduct from the southern end of the Bois de Remoulins to Saint Bonnet, such is the overgrown nature of the terrain. The only feasible off-road solution is to retrace your steps to the track that initial climbs up into Valley 9 (DFCI B53). Go past the path that leads to Waypoint 95 and shortly after the right hand bend, you will find **Waypoint 94** on the left hand side of the track. This comprises a short length of dressed stonework from the outer face of the left hand wall.

Continue up the hill and, as you climb up on to the interfluve between Valleys 8 and 9, you will gain an impression of the depth of the two valleys and the difficulty that the builders would have encountered in threading the aqueduct through them.

Walking along the interfluve you will enjoy wonderful views of Remoulins, Vers-Pont du-Gard and Saint-Bonnet-du-Gard. On a clear day Mont Ventoux is visible in the distance. More relevant to an aqueducteur, if you look to the north it is possible also to see into Valley 7 and maybe catch a glimpse of Waypoint 85, Pont de la Combe Joseph.

The course of the aqueduct is on your right, about 100 metres away and 50 metres below the track. Waypoint 102 is located somewhere on the property of Domain du Pélican but I have not been able to gain access to the property to see if any visible vestige exists there.

After walking along the track for just over 1 km, you descend into a valley. Take the path on the left and after about 400 metres, just before the path joins a paved road, look down at your feet and you will see a pair of 'tramlines' where the aqueduct crosses the path (**Waypoint 103 - Chemin du Sablas** - Photograph 33).

Photograph 33. Waypoint 103 - Chemin du Sablas

111

Unfortunately, this fragment is one of only two vestiges of the aqueduct that are visible as it passes through Saint Bonnet, the remainder having been quarried to provide building stone, destroyed by the Canal de Pouzin, or covered by more recent housing development. It is however quite easy to follow the course of the aqueduct through the village and to visit the massively fortified church which includes many pieces of reused aqueduct stone in its walls.

Continue down the path from Waypoint 103 and turn right along a farm track. The course of the aqueduct is in the overgrown area to your right and after about 100 metres it is immediately on the right of the track, as witnessed by an excavation pit, possibly the location of Waypoint 104. From this point onwards the bank left by excavations for the Canal de Pouzin will be your guide

After a further 50 metres the track turns to the right but you should continue straight on into an open area and follow the path into the field behind it. As you enter the field the excavations of the Canal de Pouzin are very obvious on your right as a bank up to 2 metres high in places. Follow the edge of the field and turn left at the end and continue until you reach Chemin de Cante Perdrix.

Turn right and after about 50 metres you will see a trench on the right hand side of the lane, this is again a remnant of the Canal de Pouzin. Climb down into the trench and after about 10 metres you will find **Waypoint 104A**, a piece of the right hand wall of the Roman aqueduct that somehow survived the 19th century excavations (Photograph 34). This vestige is approximately 10 metres long and comprises the inner face of the right hand wall of the channel complete with part of the vault and the cement lining. Also visible at your feet are some large pieces of calcretion which appear to have been removed from the wall.

Photograph 34. Waypoint 104A

You now have a choice; to follow the original course of the destroyed Roman aqueduct (a total of about 3 km) without the prospect of seeing any trace of it, or to take a short cut of about 1km.

The short cut involves turning left into Chemin de Cante Perdrix, turn left on to Chemin de l'Espeluque and then right on to Chemin du Sablas. Follow the latter to the main RN86 and cross into the centre of the village. Turn left into Rue de l'Horloge and left again into Rue Puech Marduel until you reach Rue du Sernhac where you re-join the course of the aqueduct as it makes a 90°turn to the southeast.

If you chose the follow the course of the aqueduct, the remains of the Canal de Pouzin provide a useful if unwelcome guide to its course. Climb out of the trench, cross Chemin de Cante Perdrix and follow the path opposite you with the continuation of the trench on your left and an orchard of olive trees on your right.

Continue to the end of the orchard where the path drops down into the trench and leads you to Chemin de l'Espeluque. Turn left on to the lane and almost immediately take the path on your right which travels across a field of old vines, and then a second more tended area of vines. The Canal de Pouzin and the course of the aqueduct are on your right for about 100 metres, after which the course of the latter turns to the left and crosses the field.

Continue to the end of the vines, turn left and exit the field and on to a concrete track. Turn left and them immediately right and walk along the edge of a second field of old vines, the Pouzin aqueduct remains on your right and disappears into a wooded area. Turn left and skirt round the wooded area until you reach its end and turn right to the edge of the field. The Canal de Pouzin reappears from the wooded area and forms the field boundary on your right.

At the end of the field is Chemin de Ledenon which you should cross and take the track on the right of the two that are in front of you. Follow the edge of another area of neglected vines and into a more tended area. Passing under a huge oak tree the Canal de Pouzin and the course of the aqueduct remain on your right until the end of the field where the latter makes a 90° turn to the left, now running along the end of the field. Keeping the deep pit, which maybe be yet another vestige of the Canal de Pouzin, on your right, cross into the next field and follow its right hand edge. Your route should now follow the edges of the fields skirting an olive orchard. Turn right after the last line of olive trees and passing through a wooded area until you reach Chemin de Tartiller. Turn left and follow the lane which, after some stables, follows the course of the aqueduct until it reaches the main road through Saint Bonnet, the RN86.

The course of the aqueduct now makes a 45° bend to the east as it crosses the RN86 and travels across an overgrown area before making a 90° turn to the north behind the houses on the left hand side of the Rue de l'Aqueduc.

The course of the aqueduct is quite difficult to follow for the next 200 metres but the best route is to cross the open ground adjoining the main road and make your way through the shrubbery keeping to the right of the larger of two large conifers. After passing through an old olive grove you will eventually meet a track. Turn left and go past the southeast corner of the Rue de l'Aqueduc housing estate and follow the path that runs down the back of the properties. This path follows the course of the aqueduct which then makes a sharp turn to the southeast at the junction of Rue de Garrigues Basses and Rue des Olivieres.

As mentioned earlier, housing development in Saint Bonnet du Gard has obliterated all of the previously known vestiges of the aqueduct in the village (Waypoints 106 to 109), although the modern roads do follow its course quite closely. Continue along Rue des Olivieres to the junction with Rue de l'Aubepine and Rue Saint-Guignol where the course of the aqueduct makes a gradual 90° turn back to the northeast and follows the latter.

Waypoint 106 has been lost under Rue Saint-Guignol which becomes Rue de Four à Chaud. In the corner of garden of No 180, close to the road, you will see a metal plate which covers a modern cistern which is believed to be located on top of a regard (Waypoint 107).

Waypoint 108 was previously visible on the left hand side of the road, just after the junction with Rue Jean Mace and near the red fire hydrant, but this has now been lost.

Turn left at the end of Rue de Four à Chaud into Rue des Figuiers into Place de Porche and then right into Rue de Sernhac. Waypoint 109 is said to exist in the cellar of one of the ruined properties which means that it cannot be accessed but if you look at the properties on your right you may notice large pieces of calcretions cut from the aqueduct on either side of an arched doorway.

As you pass the massive gateway to the church on the right you will see yet more pieces of striated calcretion incorporated into the arch. As was the case for the church (see below) this is an example of the re-use of materials robbed from the aqueduct. It is well worth a detour around the old part of Saint Bonnet as there are several examples of the where material from the aqueduct has been similarly re-used. Most obvious are the blocks of calcretions with their distinctive striations.

The channel is now on your right-hand side making a 90° turn to the southeast and following Rue de Sernhac before it makes a second 90° turn to the southwest to follow the lane that leads past the cemetery.

Before leaving Saint Bonnet you must not fail to visit to the church, the construction of which includes a huge amount of Roman stone robbed from the aqueduct, which passes less than 50 metres from it on three sides. Founded in the 9th century and dedicated to Saint Bonnet, it was fortified between the 11th and 14th centuries and is a fine example of a fortified church and typical of that found in this part of France. The aqueducteur may see this re-use of Roman material as sacrilegious vandalism but it is an early example of

116

recycling, several centuries before this became fashionable. By way of acknowledgement of the source of much of its stone, the design of the roof of the church also includes a crude representation of the Pont du Gard.

The course of the aqueduct now passes to the east of Saint Bonnet although there is little to be seen by way of obvious vestiges until you reach Sernhac. Once again there is a choice between following its course of the aqueduct over the fields or by taking a short cut by way of more distinct paths.

For the former option you should continue along the track that goes past the cemetery and follows the course of the aqueduct for about 250 metres before the latter makes a 90° to the east. Just before the track makes a slight turn to the right you should cross the area of fruit trees on your left until you reach the opposite corner, your path approximately following the course of the aqueduct. At the corner of this area cross into a field of vines turn right and follow the path around its edge. The course of aqueduct cuts across the field in in an easterly direction. The path becomes a farm track and after passing an open area of land on your right the track turns to the left and you are once again close to the course of the aqueduct which is hidden in the trees on your right.

At the end of the field is a high fence but you should take the path behind the fence and along the southern edge of the field, once again the course of the aqueduct is close by on your right. At the end of the fence you should follow the southern edge of an orchard of olive trees for about 200 metres until you approach a wooded area. In front of you is a path into the trees which you should follow until you reach a more obvious path where you should turn right. Waypoint

110, which is the location of a 90⁰ turn to the south, is somewhere within the trees but I have found nothing to indicate its location.

The short cut to the route given above involves remaining on Route du Sernhac until you are about 200 metres from the junction with the track to the cemetery when you should take the track on your right. The track turns to the left and then to the right at the location of a spring before turning left again. For the next 100 metres the course of the aqueduct is between 50 and 100 metres away on your right, with Waypoint 110 being located adjacent to the next left turn. Follow the track for another 10 metres and take the path on your right.

You are now heading almost due south with the course of the aqueduct on your right, sometimes only a few metres away. If you scramble up the bank on your right in the more open areas, it is possible to find evidence of the bedrock having been cut back to provide the right hand wall of the aqueduct.

At a junction with a larger track turn right and after about 100 metres, with a large cherry orchard on your left, there is a step down in the path which then turns to the right. Look ahead and to the right and you will see a distinct valley running down the hillside, this was the next obstacle that the aqueduct had to negotiate.

As with the more prominent of the valleys in the Bois de Remoulins, the mensor had to decide whether to follow the contour up and down the edges of the valley or build a structure to cross its mouth. In this case the former was chosen, and this resulted in a deviation in the course of the aqueduct that was about 50 or 60 metres.

The path now curves to the left and if you look to your right you will see a very eroded area of limestone. Climb up a few metres and you will find a 2 metre wide trench carved in the limestone at the bottom of which is some obvious stonework (**Waypoint 111**). The course of the channel can be followed for about 50 metres along the trench and, although most of the stonework has been robbed there is much evidence of the chisel marks made when the trench was carved out of the bedrock.

There is no evidence of the turn of the aqueduct at the top of the valley although the determined aqueducteur can find a short length (~10 metres) of the right-hand wall of the carved trench on the other side of the valley (**Waypoint 112**), submerged in the undergrowth. To find this vestige you should take the path up the valley for about 20 metres and climb into the undergrowth on your left. The vestige is barely 20 metres across the valley from Waypoint 111 and again its identity is revealed by chisel marks on the face of the limestone. Unlike Waypoint 111 only the right side of the trench is visible and there is no obvious stonework from the aqueduct channel itself.

Return to the main path and follow this for about 400 metres, the course of the aqueduct remaining on your right, until you reach the ancient Sernhac quarries where the tunnels were carved to allow the aqueduct to pass through a valley now called Les Escaunes.

The area in which the tunnels are located has recently been developed very sympathetically by the local commune. There are several useful information boards and a series of *'fil de l'eau'* markers which together allow you to follow the course of the aqueduct through the valley.

As you approach the first of the two tunnels you may notice that you pass through a short 2 metre wide cutting in the bedrock, this is the first indication of the course of the aqueduct through the quarried area.

The two tunnels; **Waypoint 113 - Tunnel de la Perrotte** (Photograph 35) and **Waypoint 115 - Tunnel des Cantarelles** (Photograph 36) are quite spectacular if only from the point of view of the effort that must have been involved in their construction.

Photograph 35. Waypoint 113 - Tunnel de la Perrotte

Each tunnel contains several interesting features including regards with foot holes on their sides to allow easier access, marks left by the miners' chisels, and locations for lamps still witnessed by traces of soot.

The tunnels are much larger than the aqueduct, which was built inside them, although only a few traces of the original stonework remain. What is visible are several examples of the tunnels being cut in the wrong direction, both in depth and direction, something that is unusual when we consider the usual accuracy of the Romans' work.

Photograph 36. Waypoint 115 - Tunnel des Cantarelles

The 'missing' piece of this significant deviation of the course of the aqueduct is Waypoint 114, which was a ponceau located at the western end of the valley. This was excavated in the 1980s and subsequently buried, its location is now identified by a marker where two sets of steps allow you to cross the normally dried up stream bed.

The real mystery of the tunnels is however that they do not appear to have been necessary as the aqueduct could have skirted the quarried area without the need for such a major effort. Why the mensor decided to tunnel will never be known but they now provide an interesting variation of construction for us to enjoy.

Exiting the Cantarelles tunnel you can follow the course of the aqueduct for a few tens of metres, taking the right fork in the path, before reaching a garden fence. Turn left and follow the path down to Chemin de l'Aqueduc. Turn right and climb up the hill into the village of Sernhac.

The course of the aqueduct passes underneath the village in a third tunnel which is located 5 to 10 metres underground and to the left of the main thoroughfare (Rue des Bourgades). Several regards are known to exist but only one is currently accessible, behind La Poste **(Waypoint 117 - Tunnel de Sernhac Village)**, under a glass cover and sadly rather neglected.

The underground course of the aqueduct exits the commune of Sernhac under Hôtel Domaine des Escaunes and crosses Rue des Bourgades near the junction with Chemin des Aires (D205).

6.7 Sernhac to the outskirts of Nîmes
Maps 8 to 11 - Waypoints 118 to 157

Distance: ~15 km   Walking Time: ~4 hours

Waypoint	Form	Description
118 Le Grès	VS	Twin openings of aqueduct and drainage channel
	VO	Three covered regards
118A	VS	Excavated regard and drainage channel
	VO	Covered regard
118B	VS	Excavated aqueduct channel
119 Font en Gour	VS	50 metre length of excavated channel
	VO	Ten covered regards
126	VS	Open regard with channel visible below
146 La Ponche	VO/NA	20-metre-long channel cut in limestone
156 L'Hermitage	VS	30 metre length of excavated channel, two vaulted sections

After Sernhac the aqueduct remains underground for all of its remaining course to Nîmes. It is however possible to follow the course as it passes around the former Etang de Clausonne, and through the communes of Bezouce, Saint Gevasy and Marguerittes, to the outskirts of Nîmes. Little is visible along this section apart from several covered regards and the occasional excavated section, but the determined aquaducteur can still gain satisfaction by completing the journey that the water made all those years ago.

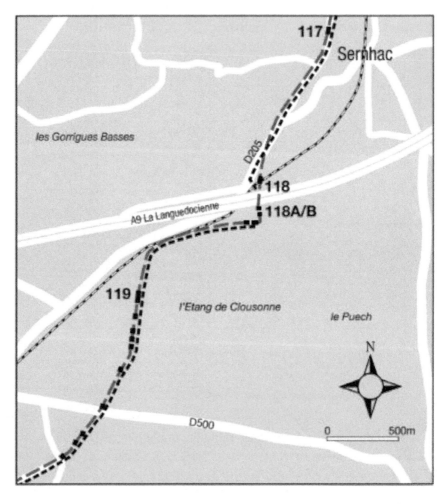

Map 8.   L'Etang de Clausonne

After leaving the village of Sernhac follow Chemins des Aires for about 400 metres, turn left and cross the bridge over the Remoulins/Nîmes railway. Follow the railway cutting back towards Sernhac for about 40 metres and climb down the steps where you will find the mouths of two tunnels which were exposed when the cutting was dug (**Waypoint 118 - Le Grès** - Photograph 37).

Photograph 37. Waypoint 118 - Le Grès

The tunnel on the right is the aqueduct and that on the left is part of the system constructed by the Romans to drain the Etang de Clausonne. The shapes of the two tunnels are significantly different with the drainage tunnel being taller and narrower than the aqueduct tunnel. The former also slopes in the opposite direction (i.e. towards the railway cutting). The other very obvious difference is that the walls of the aqueduct tunnel are coated with thick layers of calcretion whereas those of the drain are clean.

The lake at Clausonne would have provided another huge challenge to the mensor, maybe one of the greatest encountered in the construction of the whole aqueduct. In antiquity its height was 3 metres above the projected base of the aqueduct channel and avoiding it would have meant a 20 km diversion along the Via Domitia. Such a diversion would have stretched the limited fall on the aqueduct to breaking point, so a means of crossing the lake had to be found. This was achieved by draining the lake and building a platform around its edge upon which the aqueduct was constructed. A potential problem with this approach was the possibility of the lake refilling and dirty water seeping into the aqueduct and contaminating the relatively pristine spring water that it contained. This required the construction of a drainage system to prevent the accumulation of water in the old lakebed, part of this being visible at Waypoints 118 and 118A.

From Waypoint 118, return to the railway bridge, but do not cross it, instead pass under the A9 Autoroute. Immediately after the autoroute bridge the track turns sharply to the left and, after a further 150 metres, back to the right. After 20 metres the track turns again to the left and if you step into the field on your right you will find a concrete slab which covers a regard.

Walk due south across the field for about 30 metres and you will find a second concrete slab, and after a further 30 metres a third together with a deep excavation pit (**Waypoint 118A**). The excavation shows how far below the ground the aqueduct is now located. The visible stonework is a piece of the drainage tunnel and the aqueduct itself, which includes a regard beneath the slab. Only the top course of stones from the original regard is visible, which is located where the aqueduct makes a 90° turn to the west. If you (carefully!) climb down into the pit and look into the drainage tunnel you will see that it turns to the left shortly after the excavation.

About 10 metres due west of the pit is another regard cover and, after a further 10 metres, is a second excavation pit which contains a section of the aqueduct including an exit from the underground tunnel (**Waypoint 118B** - Photograph 38).

Photograph 38. Waypoint 118B

This pit is easier to climb into than the previous one and is well worth the effort. The stonework is beautiful and there are significant calcretions on the channel walls, but noticeably less than was seen in the Bois de Remoulins. One theory for this is that by the time the water had reached this point the concentration of calcium salts had been reduced due to earlier depositions.

Continue due west until you reach a line of conifer trees, you will have followed the course of the aqueduct which now changes direction to run alongside the railway, still being several meters underground. After about 500 metres the course of the aqueduct changes to almost due south and follows the edge of the field. The bank on your right is a remnant of the Canal de Pouzin, the course of which lies about 10 metres to the west of that of the Roman aqueduct.

Follow the track southwards for about 300 metres until you see a large tangle of brambles on your left. This conceals **Waypoint 119 - Font en Gour** which was excavated many years ago as part of a farmer's drainage scheme (Photograph 39). This 50-metre length of aqueduct lies at the bottom of a 4 metre deep trench and comprises the whole channel, complete with calcretions, but missing the vault. The trench includes a bridge at its mid-point, which is unlikely to be Roman, as it would have no purpose with the aqueduct channel being buried so far underground in antiquity, but it is certainly well constructed and in a vaguely Roman style.

Following Waypoint 119 is a series of covered regards, 10 in total, which trace out the course of the aqueduct as it crosses the D500. This large number of regards, some less than 20 metres apart, is not typical of the aqueduct, there only having been a few along the entire section of the aqueduct from the source to Sernhac. One reason could be that the section from Sernhac onwards has a much lower gradient and that more frequent cleaning of debris from the channel was deemed necessary.

Photograph 39. Waypoint 119 - Font en Gour

Archaeological investigations conducted over the past two centuries have shown that the aqueduct is largely intact over a distance of at least 500 metres between Waypoints 119 and 119A.

For some reason the builders of the Canal de Pouzin chose to locate their excavations parallel to, but a short distance to the right of the Roman aqueduct between Sernhac and Bezouce. This meant that they did not destroy the aqueduct in this area. Photograph 40 is an aerial view to the south of Waypoint 119 (from Google Maps®) where both channels are visible as 'crop marks', together with a number of the covered regards (marked with an 'R') of the Roman aqueduct.

129

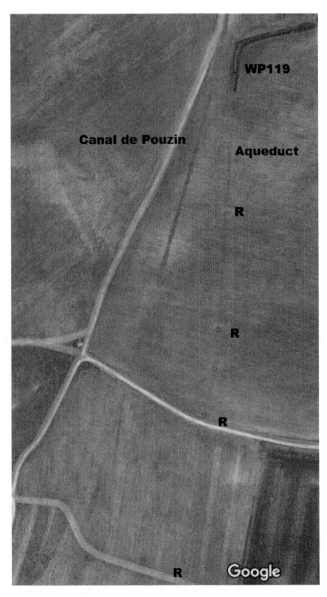

Photograph 40. Waypoint 119 Two channels and regards

After crossing the D500 follow the track that runs between two fields of vines until you reach Mas de Gleyzes, turn sharp right and then left, which will bring you outside Mas de Rogier. The course of the aqueduct passes underneath this property and there is a regard in the garden (Waypoint 119A) but this is not accessible.

As you continue along the road, the aqueduct is only a few meters from the road on your left. The Canal de Pouzin is on the right-hand side, although little remains of this either, most of the trench having been filled in. Just before the Mas de Pazac a deep drainage channel crosses the road and traces of the aqueduct can be seen on both of its banks about 5 metres from the left side of the road. At Mas de Pazac itself a further regard (Waypoint 121) exists, but this is also not currently accessible.

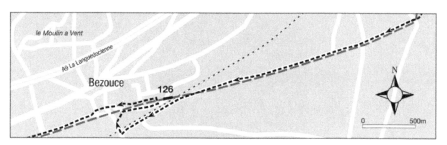

Map 9.   Bezouce

Continue along this road and after about 2 km you will reach the village of Bezouce. For this whole distance the course of the aqueduct remains on your left, and the Canal de Pouzin on your right. Once again, the latter has been filled in, but as you approach Bezouce it becomes more distinct, and its greater size when compared to the Roman aqueduct is obvious. Several excavations of the aqueduct have taken place over the years (Waypoints 124, 124A, 124B and 125) but no traces of these now remain.

131

As the road reaches the railway just before Bezouce it turns to the left but the course of the aqueduct keeps straight on, crossing the road and then the railway. Continue along the road for another 500 metres and cross the railway at the level crossing. Walk towards the Stade, turn left, and left again into the Rue de la Source.

The commune of Bezouce have created a very pleasant park celebrating the passage of the two aqueducts through the village, the Roman original and the Canal de Pouzin. This is located at the end of the Rue de la Source and is best accessed from the western end. Keeping close to the line of conifer trees on your left after a short distance you will notice a two-piece metal cover on a concrete plinth. Lift the covers and you will find a regard (**Waypoint 126**), about 6 metres deep (Photograph 41).

Photograph 41. Waypoint 126 - Regard at Bezouce

Continuing walking west and there is a *noria* constructed above the aqueduct and designed to lift water from the aqueduct and transfer it to the Canal de Pouzin via a system of gutters and inverted syphons. This interesting feature is nothing to do with either aqueduct! There are also two rows of stones that indicate the continuing course of the Roman aqueduct.

Return to Rue de la Source and walk back towards the Stade, the course of the aqueduct is on your right, underneath the gardens of a row of new properties (Waypoints 127, 128 and 129). Two regards (Waypoints 130 and 131) are known to exist, both on private property, the second being in the grounds of the Maison Londe on Rue Londes.

On leaving Bezouce the direction of the course of the aqueduct is almost due east and it can be followed by walking towards Saint-Gervasy along Chemin de Marguerittes. From Bezouce onwards the builders of the Canal de Pouzin decided that their excavations should follow the course of the Roman aqueduct more closely and this resulted in wholesale destruction of the latter.

The course of the destroyed aqueduct is initially close on your right, but it gradually curves away from the road. At the junction with the D803 turn right and you will cross the course of the aqueduct just before you reach the junction with the D6086 where you should turn left. After about 100 metres you again cross the course of the aqueduct as it travels underneath the village of Saint-Gervasy.

After about 100 metres, cross the D6086 and turn left into Rue de Ventoux. The course of the aqueduct is about 20 metres away, underneath the houses on your right. At the end of Rue de Ventoux turn right and at the roundabout turn left on to Rue de Cabriéres (D3A). You are now back on the course of the aqueduct.

At a left hand bend of Rue de Cabriéres bear right on to Rue de la Madone. After 50 metres, at the junction with Rue de Goujac, you pass over the location of Waypoint 132. The course of the aqueduct now follows Rue de la Madone past the junction with Rue de l'Aqueduc and into the field where Waypoint 133 was located. However, it is difficult to follow the course of the aqueduct beyond this point and you should continue along Chemin de la Combe, turning left on to Chemin de Souchon, which runs alongside the A9 Autoroute.

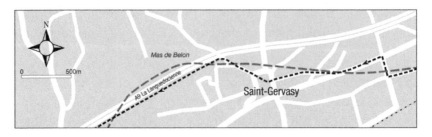

Map 10.   Saint-Gervasy

After Waypoint 133 the course of the aqueduct passes underneath the A9, although this section had already been destroyed by the Canal de Pouzin over a century before the autoroute was constructed. Indeed, from here until the outskirts of Nîmes the destruction of the aqueduct by the Canal de Pouzin was almost total. In this area alone (i.e. between Waypoints 132 and 138), almost 2 km of the aqueduct was destroyed, with a further 2 km was lost around Marguerittes (Waypoints 139 to 145). But you can still follow the course of the aqueduct, cursing the Marquis de Preigne as you do.

As you walk along Chemin de Souchon the course of aqueduct is just north of the autoroute for about 500 metres, where Waypoints 134 and 135 were located. It then recrosses the autoroute in the region of Aire de Nimes-Marguerittes and follows Chemin de Cabrieres.

Continue along Chemin de Souchon for another 500 metres, passing the locations of Waypoints 136 and 137 on your left. When you reach the D135 turn right, passing Waypoint 138, cross the autoroute and turn immediately left to follow the road that runs alongside the north side of the autoroute.

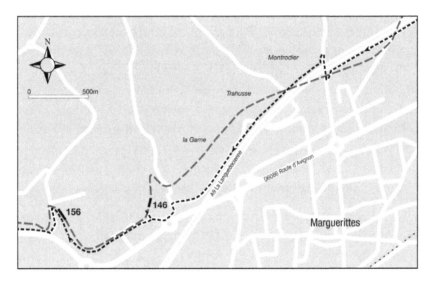

Map 11.   Marguerittes

After about 200 metres the course of the aqueduct crosses the autoroute again, near Waypoint 139, and follows the track on your right, which runs at an angle of about 45° to the main road. Unfortunately, there is no easy way to follow this section of the course of the aqueduct and the best option is to continue along the road and past the front of the dechetterie.

Immediately after the dechetterie is a road on your right, Waypoints 140 and 141 were located approximately 200 metres up this road, and on either side of it. It is possible to follow the course of the aqueduct by following the line of massive regards of the Canal de Pouzin but neglect over the years has made the path overgrown to the point of being impenetrable in places. The more sensible option is to continue along the main road for about 100 metres before taking the track on your right.

Follow this track for about 800 metres, the course of the aqueduct is about 100 metres on your right, where Waypoints 142, 143 and 144 were located. You eventually reach a small industrial estate where you should turn right up Chemin de l'Aqueduc. After about 100 metres the road turns to the right and then to the left and you see a partially restored stone and brick built section of the Canal de Pouzin. This section including a massive regard and a bridge over the stream that periodically runs down the valley of La Ponche, the same valley that made the diversion of the Roman aqueduct necessary.

Whilst the Canal de Pouzin cut straight across the valley the Roman aqueduct turned sharply to the right to negotiate the valley, the location of Waypoint 145 being located about 100 metres up the road that leads up the east side of the valley. Shortly after Waypoint 145 the aqueduct made a sharp left turn to run back down the western side of the valley, although nothing is visible here.

Retrace your path down Chemin de l'Aqueduc and follow it around the warehouses on your right until you reach a forked junction. The sensible option here is to take the left fork, La Ponche South, and follow this to the next valley. However, if you take the right fork and continue along Chemin de l'Aqueduc, it is possible, with great determination, to find **Waypoint 146,** hidden away in very dense undergrowth. If you chose this option (it took me at least three attempts before I literally fell into it) be prepared to be attacked by vicious undergrowth!

At the top of Chemin de l'Aqueduc where the road turns to the left, climb over a pile of earth on your right and into a rubbish strewn field. Keep to the right hand side until you see a sanglier track over a mound of earth and rubble and climb over it. Follow the crude path for no more than 20 metres and you will come across the stone vault of the Canal de Pouzin. In front of the vault look out for a 2 metre wide channel cut into the limestone into which the aqueduct was built (Photograph 42). Approximately 20 metres of the channel was excavated in the 1980s and although it is now almost completely overgrown, it is still visible to the trained eye.

Photograph 42. Waypoint 146 - La Ponche

Return to Chemin de l'Aqueduc, walk to the bottom and turn right along La Ponche South. The track weaves from one side to the other of the course of the Canal de Pouzin and the Roman aqueduct, as witnessed by the massive regards of the former on each side of the track, together with occasional pieces of the huge vault.

You have now reached the valley of L'Hermitage where again the Canal de Pouzin took a short cut, leaving several hundred metres of the Roman aqueduct undisturbed. The track curves to the left and just after a particularly impressive piece of vault, take the path on your right. The aqueduct first appears as an overgrown broad trench on the left side of the path before becoming a deeper more defined trench. Just before the path turns left and crosses the trench you can see the stonework of the channel clearly together with a section of vault (**Waypoint 156 - L'Hermitage**).

Photograph 43. Waypoint 156 - L'Hermitage.

The vault reappears on your right and after 20 metres there is a break in the undergrowth which gives you access to a 40 metre long section of channel (Photograph 43 and front cover). This includes a second fully vaulted section and a piece of the channel excavated to show the walls and cement lining. Again there appears to be little or no calcretion here which suggests that by this point, all the calcium salts in the water had been depleted by previous deposition.

After many kilometres of seeing nothing, Waypoint 156 is a real treat! Again it took me several attempts to find it but when I finally did it was a very special moment. This is the first opportunity since Waypoint 2A that you will have to crawl through the aqueduct channel and under the vault, don't miss it as it is also the last opportunity!

Continue along the path for another 150 metres until you reach a more substantial track, turn left and walk along the track until you reach a T-junction with a concrete road where you should turn left.

Immediately on your left is the location of Waypoint 157 where the aqueduct made a very sharp left hand turn and ran almost due south on the opposite side of the fence of the sports centre and towards Route d'Avignon. After about 150 metres at a right turn in the road the course of the aqueduct turned to the right where it was consumed again by the Canal de Pouzin.

6.8   Under the streets of Nîmes

Maps 12 and 13 - Waypoints 157 to 175

Distance: ~9 km   Walking Time: ~3 hours

Waypoint	Form	Description
160 - Mas d'Aquila	VS	5 metre length of left hand wall on side of railway cutting
161 - Impasse Wimille	VS	Section through channel set in bank
175 - Le *castellum*	VS	Base of water tower

After leaving the valley of l'Hermitage the aqueduct had to negotiate several more minor valleys formed by the streams which cut through what was formerly garrigue outside of the walls of Nemausus. For all of this final section the aqueduct was underground, although its course has been reasonably well defined by way of a series of regards, excavations and accidental discoveries over the last two centuries. As a result, the course of the aqueduct can be followed all the way to the Castellum (Waypoint 175), although only two minor vestiges are visible along the way: Waypoints 160 and 161.

From the location of Waypoint 157 walk down the road that follows the fence of the sports centre, the course of the aqueduct is on the right side of the road, behind the fence. At the bottom of the road turn right along Route d'Avignon, the course of the aqueduct remains on your right and passes under the southern end of the football pitch (Waypoint 158) before curving back towards Route d'Avignon where, after a further 150 metres, Waypoint 159 was located.

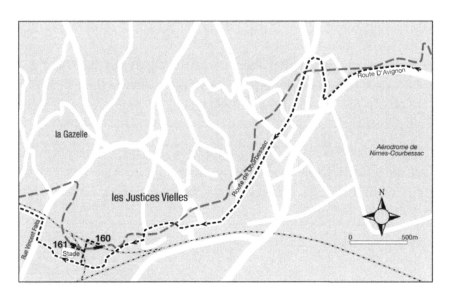

Map 12.   Eastern Nîmes

Turn right at the roundabout and on to Avenue Clément Ader. As you pass the École National de Police de Nîmes the course of the aqueduct passes under the road and Waypoint 159A was located in the grassed area on the opposite side of the road to the École.

Walk to the next roundabout and turn left down Route du Courbessac. At the junction with Rue des Mousquetaires the course of the aqueduct makes a 90⁰ turn to the left and follows Route du Courbessac for about 50 metres. It then bears to the right to negotiate the first of the three small valleys that are spread over the next 1.5 km. Continue along Route du Courbessac until you reach the railway, the course of the aqueduct being about 20 metres on your right at this point.

As Route du Courbessac turns left and passes under the railway bridge you should carry straight on to Rue Louis Armand. At the next junction you cross the course of the aqueduct. Turn right into Rue Auguste Chabaud and follow this road to its end where again you cross the course of the aqueduct as it negotiates the Valat des Justices Vielle. Turn left into Chemin des Justices Vielle and then right into Rue Henri Frenay. After about 200 metres you will reach Chemin du Serre Paradis.

Cross over the roundabout in front of you, the course of the aqueduct swings to the north to negotiate a minor valley and is under the modern houses, where Waypoint 159B was excavated during their construction.

Photograph 44. Waypoint 160 - Mas d'Aquila

After making a turn at the top of the valley the course of the aqueduct turns south and crosses the railway on your left. Vestiges have been seen on both sides of the railway cutting at a height of about 3 metre above the track bed (**Waypoint 160 - Mas d'Aguila**) but that on the north side is now hidden in the overgrown bank on your left. To see the vestige on the southern side of the cutting you should go over the bridge and turn right on to Rue Jules Verne. After about 100 metres pass under the modern railway viaduct, turn right at the roundabout on to Rue Pitot, turn right and pass under the viaduct again, and follow Rue Pitot over the railway bridge. After about 50 metres take the track in front of you for a further 50 metres where there is a break in the trees on your right. On the opposite bank of the railway cutting, you will see a 5 metre length of the left hand wall of the aqueduct (**Error! Reference source not found.**). This is not a very prominent vestige and will need some looking for, but once you see it, it becomes more obvious.

Retrace your steps and after passing under the railway viaduct turn right into Impasse Jean-Pierre Wimille. Follow this road behind the stadium and **Waypoint 161 - Impasse Wimille** is in the garden of No. 12, behind locked gates. If you are lucky Madame may be at home and would be delighted to show you a rather disappointing vestige of the aqueduct which comprises a cross section of the channel as it disappears into a bank (Photograph 45).

Return to the roundabout at the beginning of the Impasse Wimille and turn right into Rue Jean Bouin and then right again on to Rue Vincent Faita. You will find yourself opposite the headquarters of the former École d'Artillerie (now part of Nîmes University) and the headquarters of the 2nd Régiment Étranger d'Infanterie, part of the French Foreign Legion.

The course of the aqueduct now makes a sharp turn to the north to negotiate the significant valley of the Cadereau de la Route d'Uzès.

Photograph 45. Waypoint 161 - Impasse Wimille

The course of the aqueduct now turns to the southwest and runs back down the opposite side of the valley about 600 metres along Rue Vincent Faita. Waypoints 162, 163 and 164 are underneath the houses on the left hand side of the road.

Turn left and follow Rue Kleber to the junction with Rue Edmond Rostand where Waypoint 165 is located. The course of the aqueduct now follows Rue Edmond Rostand with Waypoints 165 and 166 located over the next 200 metres and Waypoints 166A and 167 on either side of the junction with Rue de Calvas.

Continue along Rue Edmond Rostand and shortly after it turns to the left you pass Waypoint 167A. At the junction with Rue Bonfa turn right. As you climb up a steep incline you will remember that water cannot flow uphill and consequently the next 300 metres of the aqueduct from Waypoint 168 to Waypoint 171 were placed in a tunnel which runs beneath Rue Bonfa in the vicinity of Eglise Saint Luc. The course of the aqueduct continues to follow Rue Bonfa for another 200 metres passing Waypoints 172 and 173 before making a 45° turn to the south.

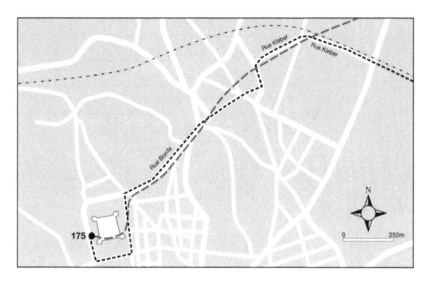

Map 13.   Central Nîmes

Turn left along Rue Vaissette and pass round the Vauban fort, now also part of the University of Nimes and under which Waypoints 174A and 174B are located. Turn right on to Rue Clérisseau and then right again after 150 metres on to Rue de la Lampeze. After 150 metres, and adjacent to the fort's western bastion you will find the base of the water tower which marks the end of the aqueduct (**Waypoint 175 - Castellum Divisorium**).

The castellum (Photograph 46), which was discovered in 1844, is a fascinating structure and is almost unique amongst the thousands of vestiges spread throughout the Roman world. The only other reasonably intact example is in Pompeii. The structure, which would originally have been covered, possibly by a domed tiled roof, comprises a circular basin 5.5 metres in diameter and 1.5 metres deep, around which was a walkway.

Photograph 46. Waypoint 175 - Castellum Divisorium

The course of the aqueduct enters the basin from the east and can be seen as an obvious rectangular opening on the right as viewed from the road. In front of this opening a sluice arrangement would have been located to allow the flow of water into the basin to be regulated. Ten large holes immediately in front of you show where the lead pipes which distributed water to the city were located. There are also holes in the base of the basin, presumably used to assist in cleaning and also to allow water to pass down the *cloacca maximus*, the city's main drain, to periodically wash it out.

146

7. A postscript

I hope that you have enjoyed reading and maybe using this book as much as I have enjoyed researching and writing it. Whether you actually 'went with the flow' or just enjoyed the walk in your mind from the comfort of an armchair is not important. Either way, James, Cookie and I have been the lucky ones, we have made our 'discoveries' and now get a buzz from passing them on to you, knowing that you have been able to share in our good fortune.

We have gained so much enjoyment along the way with many 'eureka' moments when a cry of 'I've found it!' has echoed across the garrigue, sometimes after many attempts to find a particularly well hidden vestige. Yes, we have made it easier for you, but not that easy and you will still have to search a bit and fight the undergrowth to make your own discoveries.

If you have followed the entire length of the aqueduct you will have seen a total of about 5 km of vestiges including eleven bridges in various states of repair, three long arcades, a few ponceaus, at least one regulator and several regards. Best of all, you will have walked about 50 km, much of it in the steps of the many Romans who built and maintained the aqueduct over a period of about 150 years, almost 2,000 years ago.

One of my greatest pleasures was actually finding a 'new bit' when I took my partner for a picnic and to show her what aqueducting was all about. Waypoint 49A will forever be 'my vestige' and I would love to discover how much of the aqueduct still remains buried beneath this short length of chiselled limestone (Photograph 47). So, although the aqueduct is so very well known, new discoveries are still there to be made, but only if you look hard enough.

Photograph 47. The Author at Waypoint 49A

What next? You may well ask, as I have done myself after finishing this project. There are about 600 other Roman aqueducts spread across Europe, North Africa and the Middle East, so there are plenty to choose from!

Happy aqueducting and please keep going with the flow!

Printed in Great Britain
by Amazon

75537226R20088